SELF-GIVING AND SHARING

SELF-GIVING
AND
SHARING

The Trinity and Human Fulfillment

John Navone, S.J.

THE LITURGICAL PRESS
Collegeville, Minnesota

Cover design by Donald A. Molloy; art by Clemens Schmidt.

Scriptural quotations, if not paraphrased, are from *The Jerusalem Bible*, copyright © 1966 by Darton, Longman & Todd, Ltd. and Doubleday & Company, Inc.

Library of Congress Cataloging-in-Publication Data

Navone, John J.
    Self-giving and sharing.

    1. Trinity. 2. Man (Christian theology) 3. Self-realization—Religious aspects—Christianity. I. Title.
BT111.2.N38   1989   231'.044   89-12550
ISBN 0-8146-1774-3

CONTENTS

Foreword

The pagan Aristotle knew that for happiness and well-being a person needs friends and that full human growth requires the fullness of the political community. Indeed he gives a penetrating analysis of the need and nature of both. But his horizon was limited to the small Greek city-state with its many gods—and the unknown god. He would be surprised to see the attributes he requires for true friendship (*philia*) and for the complete community (*koinōnia teleia*) stretched to their utmost by the revelation of the God he thought could neither be our friend nor communicate with us. He might also be pleased, since this new horizon opens the way for responses to many questions that remain unanswerable within his limited perspective.

Western culture has come a long way since Aristotle; but it is not clear that the presently prevailing ideology derived from Hobbes and Locke is better than Aristotle's perspective. In our weariness and isolation following more than three centuries of divisive individualism with its interminable debates, it is perhaps more than a coincidence that new approaches to "the meaning of the human person" are appearing. One is the move by philosophers, moralists, and social scientists to explore more thoroughly the notions of friendship and community. They see this as a way to break out of social atomism and retrieve some of the communitarian spirit of the Greek and medieval traditions.

A second direction lies in a new emphasis on narrative that seeks the unity and meaning of a human life in its "story," which is never just one person's story. For the story of each is bound up with the stories of all others, present and past. Inevitably by our communications, institutions, and traditions, we in fact establish some continuity and community with all humanity in the ongoing search for the good life. Individuals receive their starting point from others, present and past; and each is responsible not only for his or her own life story but, through this, for contributing to this search and thus for the future of the story of humankind. Each can find a "local habitation" within a whole that makes some sense. Life is not merely "a tale told by an idiot."

But this is not yet the whole story. Human history provides many of the middle pieces that provide some continuity and intelligibility of their own; but the story lacks a beginning and an end that could provide at least a framework for full intelligibility. Possibly this accounts in some degree for a third trend, a renewed interest in the Trinity by biblical scholars, theologians, Church historians, and others. The rise of "narrative theology," to which Father Navone has made his own contribution, is a significant step in this movement. The Trinity is now seen not just as a puzzle to be solved but as the living source from which the whole story can be grasped and lived.

Certainly early Christians, including the apostles and evangelists, understood that the human story, as well as the cosmic story, begins with God's creation, has its middle in the incarnation, and its consummation in the resurrection and return to God. St. Augustine's *City of God* is the paradigm of this view of history. What is new is the emphasis on God precisely as Trinity and, therefore, as Communion and Community. We are "made in the image of God," and God is not a monad but a family.

Father Navone's meditative and illuminating work clearly flows in this stream of continuing efforts to understand the Trinity in ways more meaningful for our life. He has described his own project well. "Each chapter of this book treats of the ways in which we become integrated into the life/love of the triune community or Blessed Trinity, ways in which the Jesus story/life becomes ours, enabling us to be our real selves together-with-all-others."

The Trinity is indeed a mystery, a secret, but one that has been revealed—in Jesus, the Son sent by the Father and, with him, sending the Spirit into the world. Our Christian creeds, our Christian commitment, are structured around this mystery. From the beginning apostles, missionaries, bishops, Christian philosophers and theologians have searched, probed, and struggled to unfold the meaning and maintain the integrity of this central message. For all reflective Christians it has been the inspiration for both thought and devotion.

Why, then, are so many Christians desultory in speaking about the Trinity? They seem to say: "It's a mystery; we can't understand it, so don't be inquisitive; just follow Jesus." But then how do you know who Jesus is and what is his way, and truth, and life? In spite of their reticence, most Christians and all practicing Catholics glimpse this secret in the words of baptism, in every sign of the cross, at every Eucharistic celebration. With the instinct of faith they know that somehow the very meaning of their lives is enveloped in this mystery. So, reluctant as they may be to talk about or try to "explain" the mystery, they do wonder and question as they worship and pray.

Father Navone is not reluctant to search into the Trinity; as he says, "A loving heart is a questioning heart." With a journey through the Scriptures he highlights the multifaceted meaning of this mystery and its implications for our lives and times. Through the Scriptures, amplified by judicious use of the riches of literature, psychology, history, and philosophy, he gives ample evidence that our search for our real self, for authentic human development and integration, is achieved only through a self-transcending love that pulls us out of our isolated self-concern and into communion and community with others, a community that is finally a communion with all men and women and with our triune God.

By creation and redemption the Father with the Son and the Spirit initiates and consummates this search. The Trinitarian community is the source, model, and goal of our communion with one another and with God. As Father Navone brings out so well, this is the model that Jesus from the cross has communicated to us by the special relation he set up between Mary, his mother, and John, the beloved disciple. In and through them this was to be the model of the Church and the call to all people.

By drawing everyone into his humanity and sonship, Jesus inaugurates a new community, the Church, which is his body and the enduring "sacrament of the Father's love for the integration of all humankind" in the life/love of the sacred Trinity. "Our ongoing Christian conversion (*metanoia*) means our learning in the Spirit of Christ to become self-bestowing persons (*kenōsis*) serving others (*diakonia*) for the fullness of life in the triune communion (*koinōnia*)."

We are constantly besieged with new theories of justice, massive legislation and legislative proposals, arms treaties, rhetorical symbols (the "human family," "dignity and worth of human persons," etc.). These are good and worthy of human efforts. But they will not by themselves solve our "social problems." Nor will a new view of the Trinity. But we must continually recall that both our human family and our personal worth have a transcendent model and value, the only one that makes human efforts fully worthwhile. And to assure such recollection there must be in the world a community in which Jesus dwells with the Father and the Spirit, a steady reminder, a sacrament, of the communion and friendship to which we are called by the Trinity.

—CLIFFORD G. KOSSEL, S.J.

CHAPTER ONE

Quest for Communion

The gospel summons us to authentic human development under the sovereignty of God's love. Our Christian conversion is both an event and a lifelong process of ongoing response to the grace and demand of the God of all humankind whom Jesus Christ as the suffering Messiah reveals to be in the service of all in establishing communion, community, and friendship among all and between them and God. Christian conversion has a universalist and communitarian dimension inasmuch as it entails transformation in every sphere of human life.

The self-surrender to God of those who adhere to Jesus Christ and his way of costly and generous self-giving service is a transforming and integrating participation in the freedom and power of God's pouring out his life for all. Jesus Christ reveals the community-creating and community-sustaining God pouring out his life for all, in and through his new covenant community. Christian conversion occurs wherever we are becoming new covenant persons giving our lives in the Spirit of Jesus and his Father for others in every sphere of human life. Christian conversion, represented by Jesus Christ's way of the cross, is a lifelong process of self-transcending love: the only way for the achievement of authentic human development and integration for *all* human persons.

We are not by nature participants in the divine nature or in the inner life of God; however, through the free gift of God's love flooding our hearts through the Spirit given to us (2 Pet 1:4 and Rom 5:5) the Jesus story/life is ours, his freedom or power to love God above all and to do good for selfless reasons is ours. His freedom or power to forgive, to reconcile, to trust and love is ours, transforming us *from* being selfish persons *to* becoming selfless persons in communion with our self-giving God pouring out his life for all. Each chapter of this book treats of the ways in which we become integrated into the life/love of the triune communion or Blessed Trinity—ways in which the Jesus story/life becomes ours, enabling us to be our real selves together-with-all-others.

The spiritual quest for communion (chapter 1) that we make in this book begins with the Good News that God has established in Jesus Christ his eschatological banquet community for all humankind (chapter 2), enabling us to find or become our real selves in communion (chapter 3). God's self-investment in human life enables and calls for our fourfold transformation or conversion for life in that community (chapter 4). Such transformation for life in the triune communion of the banquet community entails overcoming our tendency to self-idolatry (chapter 5) that we encounter in our pastoral, tragic, and melodramatic forms of experience (chapter 6). The gospel is a norm for such transformation (chapter 7); its many questions present the question-raising God and his demand for responsibility within every sphere of human life (chapter 8); its heroes, saints, and leaders are models for life in the banquet community (chapter 9). The body of Christ is the sacrament for human transformation (chapter 10), communicating the love that enables commitment in friendship and community (chapter 11), helping us to find ourselves in the life story of Jesus Christ (chapter 12), and to find our home in the community of the three divine Persons (chapter 13).

The question-raising mystery and Word of God ground our experience of radical incompleteness at every level of human life (intrapersonal, interpersonal, social, national, international), triggering our quest for the real self in communion and community. The problematics of that quest—the internal and external obstacles to communion and community—are reflected in the unified triptych of literary forms: the pastoral, tragic, and melodramatic. In terms of our need for the right models to lead us to true communion and community, the community of Christian faith welcomes Jesus Christ as God's Good News for all humankind. To be with Jesus Christ and all others in the triune communion is the fullness of life or destiny of every human person. The triune God creates and sustains every human person for that eternal communion.

CHAPTER TWO

The Last Day and the Last Supper

There are remarkable correspondences between Mark's account of the passion and death of Jesus and the messianic banquet prophecy of Isaiah 25:6-10: the mountain/Calvary; the divine initiative; the Messiah through whom God achieves his ends; the eschatological banquet/Last Supper; the universal scope of the event "for all"; the removal of the veil/tearing of the temple veil; the triumph over death; the removal of the people's shame; the divine judgment, on "that day" of God's once-and-for-all intervention for our liberation and salvation; the revelation of God and his salvation; joy in the fulfillment of all human hopes. The words of the Last Supper referring to the messianic banquet (Mark 14:25 = Matt 26:29 = Luke 22:18) look ahead to the definitive triumph of Christ's kingdom.

On this mountain,
Yahweh Sabaoth will prepare for all peoples
a Banquet of rich food, a banquet of fine wines,
of food rich and juicy, of fine strained wines.
On this mountain he will remove
the mourning veil covering all peoples,
and the shroud enwrapping all nations,
he will destroy Death for ever.
The Lord Yahweh will wipe away
the tears of every cheek;
he will take away his people's shame

everywhere on earth,
for Yahweh has said so.
That day, it will be said: See, this is our God
in whom we hope for salvation;
Yahweh is the one in whom we hoped.
We exult and we rejoice
that he has saved us;
for the hand of Yahweh
rests on this mountain.

—Isa 25:6-10

The literary-theological whole that is Mark's Gospel depicts the last day of Jesus' historical life story as the Last Day of Israel's eschatological hope for God's final coming in judgment to set all things right. The Last Day is that of a divine judgment. When God comes in judgment in such events as the Exodus, he overcomes evil and achieves a good for his people. Divine judgments or interventions are always liberation events that free his people *from* an evil *for* a good. The Last Day is the Last Judgment in which God finally overcomes the evils that afflict his people and achieves their ultimate blessedness in a once-and-for-all-event (salvation).

The Jewish day began at sunset and ended at the following sunset. Starting with the Last Supper, Mark begins the Last Day or Judgment Day at sunset (Mark 14:17). Jesus and the Twelve celebrate the Passover meal, or Last Supper, on the Last Day, recalling the prophetic tradition that the Messiah would inaugurate eschatological happiness (communion between God and humankind, and among all humankind) through the formation of his banquet community (Isa 25:6-10; 55:1-3; 65:13-14). The Last Day is the first day of the eschatological banquet. God comes in judgment to vanquish whatever evil that would stand in the way of the ultimate blessedness that he has prepared for all humankind with the establishment of his eschatological banquet community. The Last Day is the day of liberation for life in the Messiah's banquet community.

Jesus, for Mark, is the Servant of God who has come to serve and to give his life for all (Mark 10:45) in the establishment of the eschatological banquet community: "This is my blood, the blood of the covenant, which is to be poured out for all" (Mark 14:24). When Mark writes of Jesus' blood poured out for all, he is not refer-

ring merely to his physical blood, but to his life given for the transformation of all. We participate in his banquet community to the
extent that we accept his life under the sovereignty of God's love
and wisdom as our own; for, in the Jewish tradition, the blood of
any creature is its life. Jews were forbidden to consume the blood
of animals (Lev 17:10-16; Deut 12:16; 15:23), because God alone was
to be their life-principle. When Jesus offers his blood for all humankind at the Last Supper, he is implicitly identifying himself with
God as the ultimate life-principle for all humankind in communion
with God and one another. Through and in him, God is integrating all persons into the fullness of life within the eschatological banquet community, establishing an indissoluble bond between himself
and his people (cf. Zeph 9:11; Heb 9:16-21). The Last Supper recalls
the meaning of blood in Israel's official worship, where the covenant
was sealed by a blood-rite: half the blood of the victims was poured
on the altar, which represented God, half on the people. Moses ex-
plained the rite: "this is the blood of the covenant God has made
with you . . ." (Exod 24:3-8). In the Passover rite, the blood of the
lamb represented a liberation from evil: it was put on the lintel and
the uprights of the door (Exod 12:7, 22-23). In the rites of consecra-
tion for priests (Exod 29:20-21; Lev 8:23, 30) and the altar (Ezek
43:20), sacrificial blood marked them out as belonging to God.

Lambs were sacrificed twice daily in the temple at the time of
Christ, at the third hour (9:00 A.M.) and the ninth (3:00 P.M.). Mark
tells us that Jesus, the real lamb that is sacrificed for all, was crucified when the first lambs were sacrificed in the morning (9:00 A.M.)
and died when the last lambs were sacrificed in the afternoon (3:00
P.M.). These were also the times when trumpets would sound from
the temple calling the faithful to worship God in his holy sanctuary. Mark implies the meaning of Jesus' life (blood) poured out for
all by linking it with the sacrifice of the lambs in the temple. He
evokes the liberating meaning of the original Passover event when
the blood of the lambs was sprinkled on the doorposts (Exod 12:13)
to save the firstborn sons of the Hebrews from death during the tenth
plague that struck the Egyptians in an act of divine judgment. Mark
implies that God is liberating, no less than integrating and consecrat-
ing, all humankind in Jesus' service for all. Jesus communicates free-

dom *from* self-absorption *for* the fullness of life with all others—divine and human—in the eschatological banquet community.

For the religion of Israel, blood is life (Lev 17:11, 14; Deut 12:23), and everything touching life is in close contact with God, the sole Source and Master of life. This association of blood with the sacred is operative in Mark's account of Jesus' Last Day and Last Supper. Mark implies that the meaning of the Last Day and the Last Supper can be grasped in terms of the interpretation that Jesus gives to Israel's traditional blood symbolism. Jesus gives his blood as a new and sacred life-principle to liberate all humankind from evil to integrate it with all divine and human others in the new covenant community of the eschatological banquet. His life (blood) is the divine gift that liberates all human persons and integrates them in the fullness of divine and human life.

Mark's use of Passover symbolism implies that the final day of Jesus' terrestrial life is the Last Day of divine judgment. Jesus dies at the time of the Jewish Passover. The darkness that covers the earth at his crucifixion (Mark 15:33-34) recalls the ninth plague, which punished the Egyptians and brought nearer the liberation of the Hebrews: "The Lord said to Moses, 'Stretch out your hand toward heaven that there may be a darkness over all the land of Egypt, a darkness to be felt.' So Moses stretched out his hand toward heaven and there was thick darkness over all the land of Egypt for three days" (Exod 10:21-23). The darkness before Jesus' death lasts for three hours to recall the three days of the primordial liberation event. The death of Jesus, after the darkness has passed, recalls the tenth plague, the death of the firstborn (males) of the Egyptians (Exod 11:5). Through his use of parallelism, Mark implies that just as the death of the firstborn males of the Egyptians is a divine judgment to free the Hebrews from Egyptian bondage, so too the death of the firstborn and beloved Son of God is the divine judgment for the liberation of all humankind. (God's judgment in the tenth plague has a negative note of vengeance in it as a reprisal for the Egyptian slaughter of the Hebrew male children, from which Moses was spared (Exod 1:16). The death of Jesus, in contrast, is a divine judgment for the salvation of all with a Jew dying for Gentiles.) The darkness and death of Jesus recall, respectively, the ninth and tenth plagues, which, typical of all divine judgments, have a negative and a positive side: God triumphs over evil and achieves a good for his people.

Mark's word for darkness *(skótos)* is nowhere employed in the New Testament in a purely physical sense, but always in a metaphorical sense. There are those who walk or sit in darkness, who are cast into the outer darkness. Darkness has an eschatological sense. The Last Day, according to Israel's prophets, is one of darkness (Amos 9:9; Jer 15:9; Joel 2:2, 10, 16; 3:4, 16; 4:15; Zeph 1:15). The darkness represents the state of alienation or separation from God. This explains why Mark repeats that at the ninth hour (Mark 15:33, 34), only when the darkness is over, does Jesus utter his prayer from the cross (Mark 15:34 = Ps 22:1). Jesus cries out in a loud voice *after* the darkness has passed because Mark is telling us that through his death God has terminated the state of separation or alienation between himself and humankind.

Mark is telling us that God has come in a final act of saving judgment on this Last Day to overcome everything that the darkness had traditionally symbolized in the relationship between God and humankind. Mark underscores the meaning of Jesus as the new temple by having him utter a psalm of Israel's traditional temple liturgy *after* the three-hour period of darkness. (The Jewish temple liturgy took place in the light of day, and never in the darkness!) Jesus' prayer implies that God, and not the powers of darkness, has the final word about the human condition. Through his use of Israel's religious symbolism, Mark affirms that God achieves his final victory over all that the darkness represents through the suffering and dying and rising of Jesus. The eschatological darkness represents the negative side of the divine judgment: the evil to be overcome. The eschatological banquet represents the positive side: the good of universal communion to be attained. Only when we join Jesus in his total self-surrender or commitment to God (Matt 15:34), will we be free for the fullness of life in communion with all others. In attempting to be our own little gods, we shall remain in the darkness, alienated from all others, divine and human, because of the radical distortion of all our relationships into manipulative and self-serving ones. Mark's Gospel is truly the "Good News" about the gift of a different life-principle for the fullness of life in communion with all others that is available for all who are willing to meet its demands.

Mark stresses the cost of total self-surrender to the demands of God for the salvation of all (Mark 15:37), narrating that Jesus died with a *loud cry* after *darkness* (Amos 8:9) had covered the land. Mark employs two signs of God's coming in judgment, according to Joel's account of the Last Day:

> Sun and moon grow dark,
> the stars lose their brilliance.
> Yahweh roars from Zion,
> makes his voice heard from Jerusalem;
> heaven and earth tremble.
>
> (Joel 4:15-16)

Mark's narrative of the Last Day and the Last Supper implies a radically new meaning for the sacred that is symbolized by the tearing of the temple veil in two, from top to bottom (Mark 15:38). Mark affirms through the symbolism of the torn veil that God has performed a final act of destructive and saving judgment. God has destroyed all the barriers between himself and humankind; he has created a direct access to himself for all humankind in Jesus, His Son, the Beloved (Mark 1:11; 9:7). Alienation has been overcome; communion has been established. The Last Day is the key and foundation for the meaning of all days of the universal human story. That Jesus replaces the temple as the center of divine holiness is the point of the accusation at his trial: "We heard him say 'I will destroy this temple made by human hands and in three days build another, not made by human hands' " (Mark 14:58).

The belief that God is the most holy and the most separate was the basis for associating the holiness of the temple with the notion of separateness. The holiness of God's dwelling place, the temple, required separateness. Similarly, the holiness of the Holy Land and the Holy City separated them, respectively, from all other lands and cities. Even the temple, a huge edifice covering a fifth of the whole area of Jerusalem, was constructed and divided into many sections on the basis of the degree of separateness between God and humankind. The Gentiles could enter the outer court of the temple, because they too were creatures of God. However, since they did not follow the law, they were not as holy as the Jews who would enter into the inner court, a more holy and separate place. Jewish men, as opposed to Jewish women, could go one stage further to the court of the Israelites, beyond which only priests could go, to the holy place or court of the priests, the temple proper. (Jesus, a layman, could not enter this section. He was not a priest of Israel; his priesthood stems from his death and resurrection. The Letter to the Hebrews describes his as a different priesthood according to the order of Melchizedek.) As though one were ascending a series of concentric circles, one travels upward and inward toward the center of the temple, the holy of holies, God's altar and throne, wherein God is enthroned above the cherubim. This is the center of the universe. Holiness (or purity) is measured in terms of proximity to the temple or center of holiness. Only one priest at a time could approach the holy of holies to offer incense (Luke 1:9). This inner sanctuary was entered only once a year, at Yom Kippur, by the high priest (1 Kgs 8:10), who filled the place with incense to maintain the separation between himself and God.

The torn veil, for Mark, represents the ultimate theophany, the divine revelation or self-disclosure. The God whose "face" or presence was veiled within the holy of holies (Exod 33:11, 14) rips away the veil and shows his "face", manifests his presence. In his death, which culminates his mission of total self-abandonment to God in the service of all, Jesus manifests his true identity; and, for Mark, this is equivalent to God himself showing his "face." Jesus pouring out his blood for all is God giving his life to all. Jesus is the communion of God and man creating the communion of God and all humankind; he communicates his communion or interpersonal life with all others, divine and human. Mark's Last Day is for the Last Supper: the eternal communion of God and all humankind is the achievement of God's coming in his saving final judgment to pour out his life for all.

Mark's Timetable for the Last Day, the Passover, of Jesus[1]

Text time	Modern time	Reference in Mark	Event
Thursday evening (after sunset)	1800	14:17-18	Passover meal of Jesus and the Twelve. Prediction about Judas.
Thursday night	2100	14:30	Prediction about Peter, Gethsemane.
Friday, after 3 hours	2400	14:37-53	Arrest of Jesus. Interrogation begins.
Friday, first cockcrow		14:68	Peter's first denial.
Friday, second cockcrow	0300	14:72	Peter's last denials.
Friday, early morning	0600	15:1	Trial before Pilate. Temple gates open for beginning of worship. Recitation of the *Shema*, "Hear O Israel!"
Friday, third hour	0900	15:25	Crucifixion. The first lambs are sacrificed in the temple.
Friday, sixth hour	1200	15:33	Darkness begins (recalling the ninth plague and prophecies of the Last Day by Amos, Jeremiah and Joel, Zephaniah).[2]
Friday, ninth hour	1500	15:34-37	Darkness ends after three hours (three days in Exodus). Death of Jesus (recalling the tenth plague) after his loud cry (recalling Joel's prophecy of the Last Day, i.e. 4:16)[3] Trumpets call faithful to temple for the sacrifice of the last lamb. Passover feast ends when the last participant falls asleep.
Friday evening (before sunset)	1800	15:42-46	The burial of Jesus. The temple gates are closed at the conclusion of worship, which occurs only in the twelve daylight hours and never in the darkness. The Jewish day concludes at sundown. The *Shema* to be recited (Deut 6:7 ". . . when you lie down, and when you rise").[4]

The Promise of Human Fulfillment at the Mountain of God.

The promise of a universal and eschatological fulfillment for humankind at the Mountain of God inspired the prophets of Israel and enabled the Christian community to grasp and to explain the meaning of Jesus Christ and his life-giving death in Jerusalem. Key elements of Israel's prophetic tradition of the Mountain of God emerge in the gospel narratives, the good news of universal salvation.

The idea of the Mountain of God as the goal of all nations is a very ancient one that Jewish prophets may have borrowed from the Jebusite Jerusalem cult. Isaiah envisions the eschatological pilgrimage of the Gentiles to the Mountain of God (Mt. Zion): "And it shall come to pass in the latter days, that the mountain of the Lord's house shall be established in the top of the mountains, and shall be exalted above the hills; and all nations shall flow unto it; and many peoples shall go and say, Come ye, and let us go up to the mountain of the Lord, to the house of the God of Jacob; and he will teach us of his ways, and we will walk in his paths" (Isa 2:2-3, parallel in Micah 4:1). Five aspects of this pilgrimage emerge:

1. *The Epiphany of God.* The nations are expectant: "The coastlands shall wait for me, and on mine arm shall they trust (Isa 51:5). Now they hold their breath: "Be silent, all flesh, before the Lord: for he is waked up out of his holy habitation" (Zech 2:13). The visible epiphany of God occurs when the Mountain of the Temple will rise above all mountains and hills (Isa 2:2). The glory of God will be revealed to all the world (Isa 40:5). God's truth will appear as a light of the nations (Isa 51:4; 60:3); "the Lord has made bare his holy arm in the eyes of all the nations" (Isa 52:10). A standard is displayed: "In that day the Gentiles shall turn to the root of Jesse, which standeth as an ensign of the peoples (cf. 62:10), and his resting-place shall be glory" (11:10).

2. *The Call of God.* God's Word accompanies his epiphany: "God, even God the Lord hath spoken, and called the earth from the rising of the sun unto the going down thereof" (Ps 50:1). This divine

command is addressed to the Gentiles: "Assemble yourselves and come; draw near together, ye that are escaped of the nations . . . look unto me and be ye saved, all the ends of the earth: for I am God, and there is none else" (Isa 45:20, 22). Israel, as God's instrument, echoes the call: "Behold, thou shalt call a nation that thou knowest not, and a nation that knew not thee shall run unto thee, because of the Lord thy God, and for the Holy One of Israel; for he hath glorified thee" (Isa 55:5). "Declare his glory among the nations, his marvellous works among all the peoples . . . say among the nations, the Lord reigneth" (Ps 96:3, 10). The Gentiles, too, who have survived the divine judgment, proclaim the glory of God among the nations, and summon them to the pilgrimage to the Mountain of God (Isa 66:19-20). But God has yet another messenger, the Servant of the Lord, who not only restores the preserved of Israel, but whom God makes known as the light of the Gentiles (Isa 42:6; 49:6). The response to the call is:

3. *The Journey of the Gentiles.* A highway is constructed straight through the Near East from Egypt and Assyria to Jerusalem (Isa 19:23). At the same time the summons is heard in the cities of the Gentiles: "Come ye, and let us go up to the mountain of the Lord (Isa 2:3). "Let us go speedily to entreat the favor of the Lord, and to seek the Lord of hosts: I will go also" (Zech 8:21). If there should happen to be a Jew of the Diaspora returning home, ten men out of all the languages of the nations will take hold of the skirt of his garment and say: "We will go with you, for we have heard that God is with you" (v. 23). All the nations, led by their kings (Isa 60:11; Ps 47:10), stream toward Jerusalem, the throne of the Lord (Jer 3:17), in an unending procession "from sea to sea and from mountain to mountain" (Micah 7:12). Their shoulders are bent under the weight of the gifts that they bring (Isa 18:7; Hag 2:7; Ps 68:30, 32). The costly gifts the nations bring are described in the vivid imagery of Isaiah 60: the wealth of the seas (v. 5), gold, silver, and incense (vv. 6, 9), borne upon camels and dromedaries (v. 6); then come animal victims for sacrifice upon God's altar (v. 7), the costly wood from Lebanon for the building of the temple (v. 13). They bear Israel's sons and daughters in their arms as a precious treasure

(v. 6), "upon horses, and in chariots, and in litters, and upon mules and upon dromedaries, to my holy mountain Jerusalem, saith the Lord" (Isa 66:20). The gates are to be kept open day and night, "that men may bring unto thee the wealth of the nations" (60:11). Those who are left out of all the nations come year by year to the feast of Tabernacles in Jerusalem to worship (Zech 14:16), even new moon after new moon they come, sabbath after sabbath (Isa 66:18). "They shall come trembling out of their close places (Micah 7:17), bowing down" (Isa 60:14). The goal of the pilgrimage is:

4. *Worship at the World-sanctuary.* "Even them (the strangers that join themselves to the Lord) will I bring to my holy mountain, and make them joyful in my house of prayer; their burnt offerings and their sacrifices shall be accepted upon mine altar: for mine house shall be called a house of prayer for all peoples" (Isa 56:7; Mark 11:17). All the ends of the earth shall turn to the Lord (Ps 22:28); they see the glory of God (Isa 66:18) and fall on their knees before him (Isa 45:23) in the courts of the world-sanctuary (Ps 96:8). Moreover, God will cleanse their lips: "For then will I turn to the people a pure language (Heb. 'lip') that they may all call upon the name of the Lord" (Zeph 3:9). With cleansed lips they will confess: "Our fathers have inherited nought but lies, even vanity and things wherein there is no profit" (Jer 16:19), and add their tribute of praise: "For thou art great and doest wondrous things, thou art God alone" (Ps 86:10); "only in the Lord is righteousness and strength" (Isa 45:24). A description of this act of adoration is given when the Sabaean prisoners of war will be brought in chains by the Persians to Jerusalem, praying as they pass: "And the Sabaeans, men of stature, shall pass before thee in chains and fall down before thee, and make supplication to thee, saying, 'Surely God is in thee, and there is none else, there is no God' " (Isa 45:14). The worship addressed to God is accompanied by lowly homage to the messianic king (Ps 72:9-11), and to the people of God (Isa 49:23), bearers of blessing for the world (Isa 19:24). The divine response to the adoration of the Gentiles is expressed in the amazing universal blessing: "Blessed be Egypt, my people, Assyria, the work of my hands, and Israel, mine inheritance" (Isa 19:25).

5. *The Messianic Banquet on the Mountain of God.* The eschatological banquet of all nations on the Mountain of God expresses the truth that all humankind belongs to the people of God under the peaceful reign of the Messiah (Zech 9:10) and the dominion of the Son of Man (Dan 7:14). "And on this mountain shall the Lord of hosts make unto all people a feast of fat things, feast of wines on the lees, of fat things full of marrow, of wines on the lees well refined. And he will destroy on this mountain the face of the covering that is cast over all peoples, and the veil that is spread over all nations. He will destroy death for ever" (Isa 25:6-8). The communion of the banquet community as mediating the vision of God is an ancient element of biblical symbolism that runs through the Bible from beginning (Gen 3:22) to end (Rev 22:17). It is of fundamental importance for grasping the meaning of all the statements in apocalyptic literature and in the New Testament about the universal messianic eschatological banquet. In the celebration of this banquet on the Mountain of God, the veil that covers the eyes of the Gentiles will be forever rent asunder, and they will behold God with unveiled face. In all Old Testament references to the eschatological pilgrimage of the Gentiles, the goal is the holy Mountain of God, Zion, where God reveals himself. The Gentiles will be summoned to the holy Mountain for the divine epiphany. The redemption celebrated at the banquet is that of Israel, revealed to the Gentiles, who are now included in God's redeemed community. The divine eschatological banquet community is rooted in the history of the people of God.

The message of Jesus promising salvation to the Gentiles summarizes the Old Testament utterances about the eschatological pilgrimage of the Gentiles to the Mountain of God at the time of the Last Judgment: "I say unto you, they shall come in countless numbers from the east and from the west, and may sit down with Abraham, Isaac, and Jacob in the Kingdom of Heaven while the sons of the Kingdom will be cast out into outer darkness (Matt 8:11-12 = Luke 13:28-29). Jesus recalls two passages from Isaiah: "Lo, these shall come from far: and, lo, these from the north and from the west," (49:12); and the description of the banquet that the Lord has prepared for all humankind on his holy mountain (25:6-10). The messianic banquet expresses the divine redemption in which the Gentiles will feast with the patriarchs, who represent the people of God. The Gentiles are incorporated into the people of God at the consummation of all things. This note of universal salvation is implied in all the parables and sayings of Jesus that speak of the eschatological banquet. He speaks of this banquet under such symbols as the wedding feast, as the high festival that awaits the faithful and wise servant (Matt 25:21, 23), as the final Passover (Luke 22:16), as the satisfying of all hunger (Matt 5:6 = Luke 6:21). This banquet is the feast upon Mount Zion described in Isaiah, God's universal feast toward which the nations flow, where the veil that shrouds them, and the covering that blinds their eyes, shall be rent asunder.

When Matthew writes that at the parousia God will gather all nations before the throne of the Son of Man (25:31), he is employing an eschatological technical term drawn from the shepherd's usage, where all nations are depicted as a flock. The gathering of the scattered, shepherdless flock symbolizes Israel's hope of approaching redemption. Both Ezekiel (34:23-24) and Micah (5:2-4) refer to a future shepherd who will feed the sheep of God. The gospels tell of the scattered Gentile flock that is brought to Zion by God's shepherd and united with the flock of God's people (Matt 25:32; John 10:16; 11:51-52). The eschatological gathering of the nations will take place at the new Temple of God on Mount Zion.

Matthew's saying about the lamp which is not to be placed under a bushel (5:14) implies that "the city set on a hill" is the city of God on the Mountain of God whose glory cannot remain hidden. Matthew (see also Mark 4:21; Luke 8:16; 11:33) implies that Jesus is the eschatological light shining forth as the revelation of God to summon all humankind to the Mountain of God.

The eschatological pilgrimage of the Gentiles to the Mountain of God is also implied when John describes Jesus at the feast of Tabernacles (7:37-38) referring to himself as the true rock from which would flow the water of life for the world. According to the Jewish Scriptures (Zech 14:16), the survivors of all the nations will come up yearly to the Mountain of God to keep the feast of Tabernacles, whose whole ritual has as its object the prayer for rain for the coming year. On either side of the river of life flowing from beneath the throne of God and the Lamb (Rev 22:1) there grow the trees of life whose leaves are for "the healing of the nations" (v. 2). The eschatological river of life flows from the sacred rock and satisfies the thirst, first of Israel, then of the whole world.

The gospel narratives of the passion and death of Jesus resume the theme of the epiphany of God on the Mountain of God. The Roman centurion is the first person in Mark's narrative to make the full Christian confession of faith: Jesus is the Son of God (15:39). That the first Christian confession of faith should come from a Gentile symbolizes the universal scope and efficacy of the Messiah or Servant of God who gives his life for all. The centurion is the spokesman for the Christian faith and for the Gentiles who are called by God to join the Jews as the people of God. The universal revelation and call of God occurs in the death of Jesus on the Mountain of God. The tearing of the temple veil in two, from top to bottom (Mark 15:38), represents the ultimate theophany, the divine revelation or self-disclosure. The God whose "face" or presence was veiled within the holy of holies (Exod 33:11, 14) himself rips away the veil to show his "face" and to manifest his presence in Jesus Christ, the world-sanctuary in and through whom God is to be recognized and worshiped by all humankind. The temple veil no longer hides God's glory. Through the death of Jesus all humankind can see the glory of God in the crucified, who has established a new people in fulfillment of the prophecy: "My house shall be called a house of prayer for all the nations" (Mark 11:17). The eschatological banquet community is established by Jesus' giving his life for all (Mark 14:24), the life of the new people and world-sanctuary.

In John's account of the passion, the "I thirst" of Jesus (19:28) recalls the prayer of Israel, the psalms that express Israel's thirst for God: "My soul thirsts for God, the God of life; when shall I see the face of God" (Ps 42:3), and "God, you are my God, I am seeking you, my soul is thirsting for you, my flesh is longing for you, a land parched weary and waterless; I long to gaze on you in the sanctuary, and to see your power and glory. Your love is better than life itself (Ps 63:2). Water symbolizes the God for whom Jesus (Israel) thirsts, with whom Jesus is one, and whom he communicates to all through his life-giving death. The water from Jesus' pierced side (John 19:34) represents the divine life that he possesses and communicates, recalling the eschatological river of life that would satisfy the thirst of all humankind for God.

The psalm on the lips of the dying Jesus (Ps 22:1) in the passion narratives of Mark (15:34) and Matthew (27:46) recalls the eschatological prophecy that all humankind would turn to God on the Mountain of God in the world-sanctuary (Ps 22:28).

God's universal salvific will for the fulfillment of all humankind is at the heart of the symbolism of the Mountain of God in Israel's eschatological prophecies. This traditional religious symbolism and belief provide the matrix for the Christian community's understanding of what Jesus Christ has accomplished for all humankind on the Mountain of God. All the gospel narratives concur that Jesus must go to Jerusalem, the Mountain of God, to fulfill the eschatological hope and desire of Israel for all humankind.

CHAPTER THREE

The Real Self in Communion

Phenomenological and existential philosophy has helped us recognize that we cannot be understood except in terms of our relationships with the world, with other human persons, and with the divine mystery of God. These relationships are not accidental and added on to the personal self, but they reach to the very center of our being, and are intrinsic to the constitution of ourselves as persons. We are by nature open to the Absolute Spirit of God, to the finite selves of other human persons and to the material world. Any human action affecting any one of these relationships must have some effect upon the other relationships also, since each reaches to the center of our being. This is why our relationships with others have a sacramental value.

But our openness to God, to other human persons, and to the world is only partial and limited. There remains in our human situation an element of selfishness and self-centeredness that restricts the degree to which we can go out to God and to others in love and union. This is why we are in need of salvation. Christ saves the human race because he overcomes the selfishness in which we are enclosed, and he enables us to go out of our false selves to the eternal life and love of God himself. But in drawing us to our real and complete selves in the mystery of God's love, Christ breaks down the barriers of selfishness that divide us from each other. We cannot be open to the fullness of divine life and remain isolated from others.

False relationships with other persons occur if within them there is an effective denial of the further relationship of each person with God. This happens if we seek to impose ourselves upon the other in such a way as to reduce his or her freedom, or if we so affirm the self of the other as to diminish our own freedom and self-identity.

We have an eternal value, insofar as through Christ's love and self-giving we participate in the eternal life of God. Every true relationship with other persons affirms the eternal value both of ourselves and of the other. This occurs where we respect the freedom and self-identity of the other, without forgoing our own. Such a relationship forms part of our own real eternal self, and is inseparable from it.

The relationship of the human race to God established in Jesus Christ implies that every real relationship with others is both Christocentric and theocentric. This relationship of communion (*koinōnia*), as the New Testament sees it, does not originate in the human race but in God.[1] It is not a random relationship of persons coming together because they share a common interest; rather, it is the relationship or coming together of those whom God has called into communion with himself through his Son and in him with one another. The divine initiative finds its best expression in the person and in the mission of Jesus into the world as divine life and love for all. Communion with God is made possible for all human persons in the Son. In Jesus Christ exists a communion between humankind and God because he is himself God and man. Incarnation is the first moment of God's communion with humankind. But our communion with God in Christ finds its focal point in the death and resurrection of Christ, in the culmination and perfection of his human life story for all. In Jesus Christ the divine initiative calls us, communicates to us the divine life, and transforms and elevates us to the divine sphere.

The communion between God and humankind that Jesus Christ is, as Son of the divine Father and human mother, is the communion that he mediates for all who are willing to accept it. Through the gift of his Spirit, Jesus communicates his filial love for his heavenly Father and human mother (John 19:26-27). The Son's love integrates humankind under the sovereignty of his Father's love. The reciprocal love of Father and Son expressed throughout the farewell discourse of John's Gospel is the same that Jesus expresses for his mother and beloved disciple (John 19:27). The love uniting divine persons unites human persons through/in the gift of the Spirit of both the Father and Son. The kingdom of God is coming wherever persons are living in the Spirit of God's originating (Father) and welcoming (Son) love. The kingdom of God is the fullness of life in the triune communion, in the Spirit of the loving reciprocity of Father and Son.

Communion with God and with one another in the Spirit of God's love is at the heart of Christ's call to conversion. Paul reduces the Christian vocation to a communion *(koinōnia)* when he writes, "God is faithful by whom you were called to communion with his Son, Jesus Christ" (1 Cor 1:9). Luke depicts the life of the first Christians as a communion: "And they devoted themselves to the apostolic teaching and fellowship, to the breaking of bread and prayers" (Acts 2:42). John affirms that communion with Christ, leading to communion with the Father, is manifested in our communion with one another in Christ: "What we have seen and heard we are telling you so that you too may be in communion with us, as we are in communion with the Father and with his Son Jesus Christ" (1 John 1:3).[2] The Father gives the communion that the Son mediates. The communion of believers is a gift of the Father to them in his Son. Believers become heirs of this gift inasmuch as they accept his revelation in the Son and act according to the demands of love that this revelation of the Son urges. The Spirit of the Father and Son continually arouses faith and love in the believers, enabling them to respond to the demands of communion (1 John 3:24; 4:13).

The primary stress in Paul's writing on communion is on a Christocentric life, the guarantee that our lives are authentically theocentric. Paul never employs the concept for the individual sharing of someone in Christ. Our Christian vocation of communion with the Son is always a sharing in Christ with others. Pauline soteriology and ecclesiology are a question of communion in Christ with others. Fellowship with Christ is our salvation; fellowship with one another in Christ is the ideal Christian community. Communion with Christ is a present reality because the call to communion begins and develops with this life. It is a future (eschatological) reality because perfect communion in Christ with others is achieved only at the parousia. There are three aspects of God's activity in the community (1 Cor 1:9): the initial giving and call of grace that awaits our response of fellowship, the continuing enrichment/development God causes in the community, and the preparation of the community for the day of the Lord's final accomplishment of its perfection.

God's covenant-creating and covenant-sustaining initiative in Jesus Christ awaits our appropriate response in authentic fellowship *(koinōnia)*. Paul presents this human reciprocity in terms of a new openness in which there are no more barriers between the circumcised and uncircumcised, no more national or racial or sexist differences but only one fellowship, no more slave but only brother, no more condemnation to any but only salvation to all. This openness allows pluralism of thought and undertaking (Gal 2:9, 10). The new openness achieved in Christ is worked out by the dynamism of his Spirit, which draws us away from an egocentric to a Christocentric realm of life in God (Phil 3). Christ's Spirit frees us *from* egoism (the "works of the flesh") *for* loving communion with the Father and with one another in Christ. The Spirit impels us to serve in love. It imparts fellowship, moving us always to the Son and Father and sustaining us in our fellowship with them. The Spirit gives continuity and growth to the present fellowship; it impels us to become more conformed to the Son for the ultimate perfection of fellowship in the glory of the parousia (Phil 3:10, 20).

This dynamic and loving openness to one another in the Spirit of Christ authentically witnesses (Acts 2:47a; 5:13) to the world constantly inviting it to the fellowship of universal love that is salvation.[3] Such fellowship (salvation) is always the gift and achievement of the Father through the mediation of the Son and the efficacy of their Spirit. Humankind, apart from the self-gift of the Father in the Son and their Spirit, cannot attain such fellowship or perfection. The call of the Father in the Son requires a power that humankind does not possess by nature. The disciples, amazed at Jesus' saying that it is hard for the rich to enter the kingdom of God, ask, "Who then can be saved?"; and Jesus answers, "With men this is impossible, but with God all things are possible" (Matt 19:23-26). Peter recognizes the Messiah only through the special revelation of the Father (Matt 16:16-17). We are called to fellowship in the eternal life and love of the Father and Son and Spirit, to something infinitely beyond the unfolding or development of our natural endowments given in creation.

The blessings of the Christian community may be thought of as an inheritance of which we are joint heirs (Rom 7:17; Eph 3:6; 1 Pet 3:7). In this context, we are partners or joint shareholders (Phil 1:7; Rev 1:9) with our fellow Christians. We share the same Holy Spirit (2 Cor 13:13; Phil 2:1), body and blood of Christ (1 Cor 10:16-18), gospel (1 Cor 9:23), faith (Phlm 6), suffering (Phil 3:10) and consolation (2 Cor 1:7), patient endurance that Christ brings (Rev 1:9), future joy (1 Pet 4:13), grace of God given in Christ Jesus (1 Cor 1:14). Paul stresses that all these blessings which unite us in fellowship are gratuitous or grace, and he never thinks of them apart from Christ, the embodiment of all that grace signifies. Through "the grace of our God and the Lord Jesus Christ" (2 Thess 1:12), we are called to a further generosity to others.

The blessings of God in Jesus Christ should inspire a sense of gratitude and thanksgiving toward God. In fact, our generosity manifests the grace of God. Paul praises the Churches of Macedonia for their joyful generosity to the poor in the Church of Jerusalem. God's grace elicits this spontaneous response of helping the needy (2 Cor 8:4, 9, 16; 9:15). Paul gives thanks for the grace of God that is operative in the generosity of service to the poor in Jerusalem (2 Cor 9:15). God gives his gifts to establish, sustain, develop, and restore a divine and human fellowship (koinōnia) without limits; for, although we are communitarian by nature, we cannot achieve the perfection of our nature apart from its ultimate origin and ground and destiny.

God's first negative reflection on humankind, recorded in the Bible, is that it is not good for us to be without others. If we have been created as knowing and loving subjects, we would be absurd without others to know and love. Persons are interpersonal, knowing and knowable, loving and lovable. The first word of God in the Bible to the human person, "Where are you?" (Gen 3:9), implies that we have been created response-able, interpersonal, cognitive-affective subjects whose perfection consists in the authentic communicating of divine and human fellowship. We are communitarian by nature, conceived and born in and through human community. We are interdependent. We are nurtured by community and in turn nurture community. Our personhood is constituted by relationships with divine and human others. Our questioning implies that we are relational. Our questions about God express our attempts to understand ourselves; for the way that we understand Ultimate Reality defines the way that we understand our relational reality.

Our questions about Jesus Christ express our attempts to understand our Christian discipleship; for the way that we understand the Master defines the way that we understand our relational reality as disciples. Love motivates the question-raising and question-answering dynamic of the New Testament writers' response to the needs of the Christian community. The Gospel narratives are implicitly the Christian community's response to the question, "What does it mean to love God with one's whole heart and whole soul, with all one's mind and all one's heart and all one's strength?" (Mark 12:30). What does it mean to fulfill the new commandment of Jesus, "Love one another as I have loved you?" (John 15:12). How do we, the Christian community, respond to that love? God calls us to find our real selves in his fellowship-creating and fellowship-sustaining love for all others. God is depicted as searching and calling for us ("Where are you?") in order that we might find our real selves in communion with him and one another.

Luke tells three consecutive parables (Luke 15) of God's searching and longing for us and of his rejoicing with all others whom he calls together in fellowship when he has found us, and we have implicitly found our real selves.[4] Homecoming, in the third parable of the Prodigal Son, is finding our real selves in joyful fellowship with God and neighbor. Our homecoming or salvation is not a solitary and exclusively private event or process. The fellowship of the Christian community is the sacrament of our homecoming or salvation. And the homecoming or salvation to which we are called is a corporate fellowship that the Father gives in the Son and their Spirit, transforming our relations to relations of love on all levels. We are called to transform all our interpersonal life into relations rooted and grounded in the love we receive in the outpouring of the Spirit of the triune communion. God's self-giving enables us to give ourselves in love.

The Church is a communion, sacrament, and communication whose inmost nature resides in the very life and being of God, Father-Son-Holy Spirit, shared with human persons.[5] The triune God is the transcendent condition of the possibility of the existence of the Church and its historical founder, Jesus Christ. This outward sharing originates in creation: cosmic and human nature as the image and likeness of God; continues in salvation history; intensifies in the incarnation of the Son and Word in an historical human nature; matures in the Church, the temple of the Holy Spirit in the human story; consummates in the new heaven and earth of the celestial city.

The Church is the history of the triune God's communion with humankind. The inward communion of God, Father-Son-Holy Spirit, enables the outward communion of God with human beings. God's inward communion becomes an actual communication with human beings, whence results the Church; the Church within itself as the people of God; the Church, as the sacrament of salvation, with all humankind.

The Church is a gathering together of people whose specific identity is provided by its relationship to God. This people's identity depends on the nature or identity of the God whose people it is. By its relationship with Christ and his Father and their Spirit, the Church is a sacrament or sign of God's internal communion; it is also an instrument for the achievement of our intimate communion with God and of the unity of all humankind. The graced life of Christian fellowship is already an anticipation and pledge of the eschatological fulfillment of this life.

The fellowship of the Church and salvation can be understood only in relationship to and in the context of the triune God, the Father-Son-Holy Spirit, who is its origin, its pattern, and its fulfillment. God-in-himself is truly God-in-us. The doctrine of the triune God discloses that the perfection of being in God is not to be in isolation from, but to be in relationship with. For divine and human persons, to be is to be with. Jesus' very being is the communion of the divine communion with the human communion (1 Tim 2:4-6). Letting God be God means letting the communion being of Father-Son-Holy Spirit become ours.

The Church is the sacrament of the triune God's intimate, joyous communion. From the overflowing communion of God within comes the communion of the Church. The transcendent communion of Father and Son and Holy Spirit becomes immanent in human history. The Church is communications; it exists to bring all human persons into communion with God in Christ and thereby to open them up to communication with each other in the Spirit of the Father and Son.

Triune Communion in John's Gospel

That love which endures forever, in John's Gospel, is a way of being and doing and seeing with others that is revealed in the life and death and resurrection of Jesus Christ. His interpersonal life with the Father and their Holy Spirit reveals that God is a community of three persons in love.[6] Their communion of interpersonal love is the "eternal life" of which John writes that transcends mere immortality. There is a Trinitarian import in John's account of the passion and death of Jesus which underlies his affirmation that God is love.[7]

The Father and the Son, for John, are neither seen nor experienced apart from one another; for seeing the Son is seeing the Father. They are simultaneously known, in the full biblical sense; and they are known in what they are simultaneously doing. The loving Father is seen in his giving his life to his Son; the Beloved Son is seen in his receiving his life from his Father. The community of Christian faith knows the Father and the Son as two distinct and equal Persons in their reciprocity of one life and love, their Holy Spirit, given to the community.

John's account of Calvary implies that the Father and Son are seen in the giving and receiving of their Spirit (life and love) that unites John and Mary to one another in the dynamic of their triune communion. The reciprocity of the Father and Son is manifested in the reciprocity of the mother and son. The dying Jesus imparts his Spirit to his mother and beloved disciple. By communicating to them the love and life that he and his Father share, Jesus enables their new way of being and doing and seeing with others. Through the transforming gift of the Spirit of the Father and Son—the triune communion of eternal life and love—Mary sees John as her son and John sees Mary as his mother. They experience themselves in the triune communion of love as being given to one another. They are one in the life and love of the one interpersonal God, while remaining distinct persons within that eternal life and love of the three distinct Persons. They accept and identify themselves in that dynamic of the triune communion of interpersonal love transforming their being and doing and seeing.

Just as the Father is seen in the Son, the Father and Son are seen or experienced in the living and receiving of their Holy Spirit, of the life and love that unite them and the community of Christian faith. John and Mary at Calvary are the Fourth Gospel's icon of the triune communion. The Son, whose filial love unites him to his heavenly Father and human mother, reveals the Father and what they are doing when he gives his mother and beloved disciple to one another. The Son imparts his Spirit—the eternal life and love that he shares with his heavenly Father—to them to enable them to become what he and, implicitly, his Father have called them to be for one another in the triune communion of love. John and Mary represent the community of faith that lives in that Spirit and prays the "Our Father" knowing that they have been given to one another by the Father and Son through the gift of their Spirit. In the real love that we have for one another, we know the triune love of Father and Son and Spirit; we live in the Spirit that is the love Father and Son have for one another.

If the Holy Trinity does in our lives what it does in its own interior life, the Father in you is giving himself to the Son in me and the Father in me is giving himself to the Son in you. The Son in you is welcoming life from the Father in me and the Son in me is welcoming life from the Father in you. We are bonded as brothers and sisters by and in the Spirit of the life-giving Father and the life-welcoming Son. We are given to one another in and through the Spirit of the love-giving Father and his love-welcoming Son, the Beloved. We know or "see" in the reciprocity of love within the Christian community the Spirit of the Father's and Son's love that has been given to us.

Intrapersonally, the three Persons are present and active and communicating in individuals, relating them interpersonally and socially. "Brother" and/or "Sister" might describe the Holy Spirit in this sharing of the triune communion; for we are bonded together as brothers and sisters through participation in the giving and welcoming of the Father and the Son. Each is Father and Son and Brother/Sister for the other. Each contributes to and benefits from the life and love of the other through the bond of the Holy Spirit given to us. We know the triune God in our interpersonal, interdependent, loving fellowship. We come to maturity through the deepening of our relationships in the triune communion through which we are nurtured and nurture one another freely, cooperatively, peacefully.

Letting God be God means letting the triune communion become operative in our lives at every level—intrapersonal, interpersonal, social, national, international. We participate in the triune communion of covenant-creating and covenant-sustaining love to the extent that we allow (1) the Father's originating love in ourselves and in others to originate that love, respectively, in others and in ourselves, and (2) the Son in ourselves and in others to welcome that love, respectively, from others and ourselves.

Mary and John are the historical counterparts in the New Testament community of covenant love to the Father and Son in the triune communion of eternal love. Just as the love originating in the Father is eternally welcomed by the Son and shared in their Spirit, so the same Spirit is understood as actively present and sustaining in the community of new covenant love as the originating love of a mother and the originated love of a son (beloved disciple). The Spirit of the Father and Son is known, in the biblical sense of a lived experience, in the giving and welcoming of their love within the covenant community, the matrix of Christian conversion as both an event and a lifelong process. The Christian community reflects the unrestricted love of the triune communion in its universal mission. It manifests and proclaims that its God is a communion of divine Persons, summoning all humankind to communion and fulfillment in its eternal love.

The universal human story would be incomplete without your/my life story. Similarly, your/my life story is meaningless apart from the universal human story. The authentic love that is given and received/welcomed among persons within the universal human story is the validating sign for Christian faith of the triune love that is God's interpersonal life. To live and love in the Spirit of the Father and the Son is to know even now, within the limits of our human finitude, the most excellent way of being and doing and seeing with others. It is a way of seeing God in all others, even in the darkness; for even loving our enemies falls within the scope of the gift of God's unrestricted and universal love given to us in the triune communion. It is seeing God as he truly is (in love with all others) and others as they truly are (beloved of God) within the historical particularities of the universal human story. All are lovable because God loves all and is with all (Emmanuel). The triune communion of Father and Son and Holy Spirit embrace all as their common origin, ground, direction, and destiny. The Christian community proclaims, celebrates, and communicates the Good News of the triune communion: the Father has sent his Son and their Spirit to draw all forever into the fullness of their interpersonal life and love.

Befriending Communion

Titus is told that in sending his Son among us, God has shown himself the "friend of humankind" (Titus 3:4). As Word of his Father's befriending love, Jesus tells his disciples, "I no longer call you servants, but friends" (John 15:15).[8] The triune communion is that of a befriending love that Jesus expressed in both his compassion and passion, a love that knows no limit or exception, "When we were reconciled to God by the death of his Son, we were still enemies . . ." (Rom 5:10). The Persons of the triune communion are not closed inward, each upon itself, but opened outward toward one another; and only thus do they remain Persons. They communicate in complete spontaneity and fullness. The whole of what the Father has he communicates with the Son; the whole of what the Father and Son are they communicate with the Holy Spirit. The perfection of human personhood occurs in the actual love of authentic friendship's giving and receiving. The triune communion is not exclusive; it is all-inclusive and works for the integration of all humankind. Just as the family that works, works for the benefit of society, so, too, the friendship that works expresses the same triune pattern of working for others. From the communion of the triune God comes the communion of the Church, the sacrament for the integration of all humankind in friendship under the sovereignty of the triune God's love.[9]

There has been a rather long tradition in Western spirituality, owing to Neoplatonic influences, Jansenism, and an excessive spiritual individualism that concentrates exclusively on saving one's own soul, which has tended to treat friendship as either a danger or a means to an end.[10] More recently, partly on account of the recovery of biblical studies, the communal nature of Christianity has been freshly reasserted. Far from being a means to an end, the fostering of real love in friendship is seen as a major object of evangelization. But such love is not to close one off from others; rather, it is dynamically apostolic and calls one to go forth and broaden the circle of communion, to draw others into the fellowship. We do not become friends as a means to save our own souls. Friendship is not a means to an end; it *is* the end. But it goes beyond itself, in apostolic love. As such, friendship and love between Christians become a powerful sharing of the Good News. Seeing how they love one another draws people to the same end, to the Gospel and faith in Christ, to the triune communion.

Dangers accompany friendship as they do any form of love—dangers of egoism, either individual or interpersonal. But the alternatives to friendship—alienation, isolation, rejection, and even divorce—are hardly Christian ideals. They are human tragedy.

The development of interpersonal relations in friendship expresses the deepest and most profound aspects of both personal and ecclesial development. As noted, it is not the means of either personal or ecclesial development; rather, it is the very flowering of that development itself. Partly for this reason the family is traditionally referred to as a "domestic church." Further, by its very nature, Christian friendship is apostolic; it is not inward-turning or egoistic, but outward-looking, basing itself on humanity's relation to Christ. From that incorporation in Christ and the triune communion derives the apostolic imperative to draw all to whom one is related into Christ himself.

Because the essence of friendship is communion, friendship involves the interplay between revelation and acceptance. Revelation of oneself to another is a gift to be accepted by both sides. These correlatives clearly illustrate the meaning of existential openness. That is, being open is not something we do at once; it is gradual and grows out of the gift of self and the response to that gift. And it is not merely a matter of talking, for speech often reveals less than action, though it intends to hide nothing. One hides oneself most of all when one's actions are contrived and one is not doing what one authentically wants. In Christian friendship, discovery of the sinful side of another ought not to lead to rejection but rather should lead to an understanding of the further potential transformative power already in the relationship. Patient love sustains Christian friendship.[11] We bear one another's burdens with the unconditional love that hopes in God for our ultimate liberation from them.

Patience is not weakness or fatalism; rather, it is the sustaining power of an invincible love and hope in confrontation with evil. Because we are limited and leave something to be desired that God alone can fulfill, patient and forbearing love is the condition for the possibility of friendship. Communion (marriage, community, society, etc.) disintegrates with the refusal to endure limitations and deficiencies in others. Our incapacity for friendship (marriage, etc.) is related to our unwillingness to be committed to others who do not fully gratify, support, or console us. The passion and death of Jesus reveal the patient love of the triune communion, which endures all things in its commitment to saving the world. Significantly, all that the Lord's Prayer has to say about interpersonal relations is that we must forgive offenses. To forgive offenses is to have life in the invincible love of the triune communion.

The nature of friendship is found in personal indwelling and communion; as such, it is the goal of evangelization. The good news is that we can have the fullness of life in the triune communion. Friendship and marriage are primary images that Jesus employed in preaching the gospel. Christian friendship calls for a reordering of our needs and expectations, a transcendence of egoism and utilitarianism. Further, it is apostolic: it tends to be open and universal rather than particular and exclusive.

In drawing us out of our selfishness to the triune communion of eternal friendship, Christ liberates us from the isolation of self-enclosure and brings us to our true reality in the fullness of his interpersonal life with his Father and Spirit: the origin and ground and destiny of all human persons. The saving mystery of God as Father and Son and Holy Spirit is both the communication to us of the inner life of God's triune communion—God's self-communication to us—and an invitation to us to enter into that life, drawing us into everlasting communion. The Church is the coming-to-visible-expression in the historical human community of the beginning of this everlasting communion with the triune God. The Church lives with the confident trust that the love of the triune God, which is already experienced as the force and inspiration of Christian life, is actively reconciling and saving the world (2 Cor 5:17-20).

The mutual love (authentic friendship) of the disciples manifests the love of the triune communion. The perfection of human persons united in mutual love communicates and reveals the perfection of Jesus Christ's interpersonal life with all divine and human others (John 13:35). The self-giving love of the Christian fellowship (koinōnia) is that of the triune communion. The ultimate and supreme human perfection is in the divine self-giving uniting us in love with all others. All human persons have an eternal "togetherness" (koinō-nia, in the cognitive-affective life of the triune God.[12] We are all known and loved together in the triune communion that is our origin, ground, and destiny. We are free to accept or to reject our real selves, our real origin and ground and destiny of universal love within the triune communion. We are free to accept or to reject ourselves as we truly are: as known and loved together in the triune communion. Doing God's will means loving ourselves and others as God loves us: as we truly are *together with all others* in the triune communion. Eternal frustration or "hell" is endlessly being at odds with our real selves in refusing to accept our real selves in our real togetherness with all others in the triune communion that creates and sustains and brings to perfection our eternal togetherness.

God wills/loves us in our togetherness with all others. We are together-with-all-others because that is the way the triune God wills/loves us. We are free to accept or to reject God's will/love, the image of the triune communion of universal love in which we have our origin and ground and perfection. The Good News of Jesus Christ is that we are known and loved together in the triune communion: who we truly are. We truly love ourselves when we welcome Christ's news and call to universal love by loving ourselves as we truly are: together with all others in the triune communion. Through the gift of the Spirit of the Father and the Son, the life of the triune communion, we are called and enabled to love ourselves truly as we are and are loved in that triune communion: together with all others.[13]

The communion of the Christian community reveals and communicates the Holy Spirit of the self-giving Father and his self-giving Son integrating humankind within the triune communion of the triune God. Christ crucified is the icon of the loving outpouring of divine and human life in the reciprocity that constitutes such communion *(koinōnia)*. He is the icon of the divine and human selflessness in communion with all divine and human others, willingly paying the price that such communion entails. There can be no communion *(koinōnia)* without selfless self-giving *(kenōsis)*. Death itself cannot quench the invincible Spirit of love that is the eternal life of the Father and Son in the triune communion. That Spirit is always a gift, the triune God's self-gift and call to our real selves in the fullness of divine and human life with all others, enabling us to do and become what would otherwise be humanly impossible. Because God alone fully loves all others, good and evil, only the gift of his Spirit enables us to love all others with the love that no human evil or death itself can quench.

Our receiving the Holy Spirit of the triune God is not passive. The mother and faithful disciple stand by the crucified Christ, actively welcoming his love commandment and the gift of his enabling Spirit. We are never more fully alive and intensely active than when we love God with our whole heart and mind and soul and our neighbor as ourselves within the triune communion enabling such love. The Christian community, the body of Christ, is the living icon of the triune God when it stands faithfully by its crucified Lord actively welcoming the gift of his Spirit in obedience to his call to the fullness of life in the triune communion. The gift of the Spirit enables the Christian community to follow its crucified and risen Lord's way of the cross, the way of selfless, self-giving love that culminates in the resurrection of the just for the fullness of life in the kingdom of the triune God. Eternal life is loving ourselves truly as we are and are loved in the triune communion/God: together with all others.[14]

CHAPTER FOUR

Conversion for Communion

Affirming that we achieve authenticity in self-transcendence, Bernard Lonergan makes conversion a central theme in *Method in Theology*. We are called to the realization of self-transcendence in terms of intellectual, moral, and religious conversion. Religious conversion, for Lonergan, is most vital, central, common, and foundational. Without it, a sustained and perduring moral conversion is a *de facto* impossibility. Similarly, without religious and moral conversion, a fully developed intellectual conversion that enables us to arrive at a critically grounded natural knowledge of the existence of God is for all practical purposes an impossible achievement.

Lonergan distinguishes between moral and religious conversion because he believes in the need to distinguish between nature and grace. We are, for Lonergan, by nature intelligent and morally oriented. We are not, however, by nature participants in the divine nature or in the inner life of God but only by the free gift of God's love flooding our hearts through the Spirit that is given to us (2 Pet 1:4 and Rom 5:5).

More specifically, we are capable of rising to various levels of self-fulfillment or self-transcendence. We are capable by nature of achieving cognitive self-transcendence in going beyond what is merely imagined, what simply appears to be so, to what in fact is the case. To know what really and truly is so is to get beyond the subject, to transcend the subject, and to reach what would be the case even if the particular subject in question happened not to exist. We are similarly capable by nature of achieving moral self-transcendence in moving beyond being dominated by desire and fear, pleasure and pain, more self-satisfaction and self-interest, into a state of commitment to true value. Moral conversion is a state of self-transcendence in which we become motivated primarily by values rather than satisfactions. We move beyond merely personal tastes and interests to become principles of beneficence and benevolence and capable of genuine loving or responsibility. We are not, however, capable of *achieving* total self-transcendence or religious conversion. Rather, we receive this type of ultimate self-transcendence as a gift. It is an other-worldly state of being in love with God that occurs within this world but goes beyond it, in which all values are placed in the light and the shadow of transcendent value (God): in the shadow, for God is supreme and incomparable; in the light, for God is originating and all-encompassing goodness. Religious conversion is a state of an unconditional being in love, since no finite object or person can be the object of such an unqualified love. Only to God can we truly say: "Without you I cannot live, love, or exist." This type of statement to another human being, if truly meant, is idolatrous. God alone can be the object of a love that is without reserve or unconditioned in every respect.

For Lonergan, conversion is foundational for community. Conversion may be intensely personal and utterly intimate, but it is not so private as to be solitary. It can happen to many, and they can form a community to sustain one another in working out the implications and fulfilling the promise of their new life. How does this community interrelate the individual and the world?

The four New Testament words—*metanoia, kenōsis, diakonia,* and *koinōnia*—may be used to represent four dimensions of conversion that complement Lonergan's thought and help us to answer the question about the integrating character of Christian conversion.

1. Metanoia: Conversion as Human Transformation

The biblical presupposition of the call to repentance and personal transformation is that human authenticity is a question of covenant living. The demands and responsibilities of covenant/community living are the precondition for knowing God in the biblical sense of doing his will. The God of Israel and Christians is a covenant/community-creating and covenant/community-sustaining God. Sin is the failure to fulfill the demands and responsibilities of covenant/community life. Conversion is the event and process of overcoming this failure to assume one's responsibilities toward God and neighbor as an authentic covenant/community person. *Metanoia* as personal transformation does not occur in isolation, apart from integration within the life of a covenant community. Persons are interpersonal. Authentically human life is relational.

Both Jewish and Christian Scriptures communicate God's Word, the acceptance of which entails a transformation on the part of the hearers into authentic covenant/community persons. The religious community employs its Scriptures to create and cultivate a community of persons who accept their responsibilities for covenant/community life. Christian preaching and Scriptures proclaim religious conversion, thematized under the rubric of becoming a disciple of Jesus within his new covenant community as the authentic fulfillment of our humanity. This fulfillment is also presented as redemptive, that is, as the solution to the evils that jeopardize authentic covenant/community living. Paul, for example, occasionally drew up lists of the traits that sealed individuals off from one another by attitudes that make community impossible. These "vice-lists" appear in Rom 1:29-31; 13:13; 1 Cor 5:10-11; 6:9-10; 2 Cor 12:20-21; Gal 5:19-21; and Col 3:5, 8. All overlap to some extent, and so they may best be indicated by drawing up a simple alphabetical list: anger, arrogance, blasphemy, carousing, conceit, contention, contriving evil, covetousness, deceit, disobedience, dissension, drunkenness, faithlessness, foolishness, God-hating, haughtiness, homosexuality, idolatry, immorality, jealousy, licentiousness, malignity, murder, obscenity, pederasty, villification, sectarianism, selfish ambition, silliness, sexual passion, slander, sorcery, stealing, swindling, tale-bearing, lovelessness, mercilessness, unruliness, viciousness, wickedness.

The Jewish and Christian call for personal transformation at every level of human life envisions the human person as relational with a life that is intrapersonal, interpersonal, social, national, and international. What happens in any one sphere affects the other spheres of our relational existence. Irresponsible decision and action in one sphere harm the other spheres, whereas responsible decision and action in one sphere contribute to the well-being of the whole. Although God transcends all human life and its spheres, he is immanently present and active in his grace and demand within every sphere of human life. The call to conversion is a demand for responsibility before God for human life in every sphere. (The Johannine "world" without God rejects such responsibility, asserting its autonomy and independence in self-idolatry.)

Personal transformation in religious self-transcendence is both an event and a process that overcomes the temptation to idolatry in every sphere of human life, to make myself or any other finite good (family, friends, class, race, nation, and so on) the supreme value of my life, to restrict my love to what is confined or limited. Loving the Supreme Good that transcends every finite good is transcending myself in the ultimate capacity for self-transcendence. It is the experience of a freedom from restricting our love at every level to a limited value or good, from the distortion that follows upon a love that substitutes the relative for the Absolute, the part for the Whole or all-encompassing Good. Conversion must occur in every human sphere.

Idolatry is the root or basic sin that is well understood in the Bible as differing from the true worship of God in the fact of its personification or objectification of the human will in contrast to the suprahuman transcendence of the true God. When an idol is worshiped, we are worshiping ourselves, our desires, our purposes, and our will. As a consequence we are outrageously guilty of giving ourselves the status of God and of exalting our own will as the supreme worth.

In the commonsense religious expression of the New Testament, death means more than simply the cessation of biological activity. Death connotes the effect of our failure to develop, of our infidelity to the exigencies of self-transcendence or conversion. It connotes the loss of our humanity on the individual and social levels. In the symbolic language of the New Testament, Jesus Christ's acceptance of death out of love has a transforming power for all humankind. Jesus accepts death, the death involved in the negation of the undeveloped, biased, and distorted self to be transcended, to transcend it in the self-transcending love that is the new life he communicates, the fullness of human living flowing from fidelity to the demands of complete conversion. The authenticity of our response to Jesus' injunction to love God above all finds its measure in the deeds by which we follow Jesus in self-transcending love for others; for only in loving God above all are we free to love others (without manipulative self-idolatry) with God's love for them.

2. Kenōsis: Conversion as Generous Self-giving

Christ begins his mission in Mark 1:15 with a call to conversion *(metanoia)* for life in the kingdom. Conversion demands human transformation for life in communion *(koinōnia)* or community or friendship with God and all others in fulfillment of the Great Commandment, the imperative of divine love for the fullness of our lives; hence, it entails our self-giving *(kenōsis)* or generosity toward God and other. There is no *koinōnia* without *kenōsis*. E.L. Mascall contributes to our grasp of this dimension.

E.L. Mascall's letter to the editors of *Theology* (May 1983, Vol. 76, no. 711, pp. 206f.) on the exegesis of St. Paul's passage in Philippians 2:5-11 represents a convincing understanding of *kenōsis*. Mascall affirms that while Paul is explicit about the personal preexistence of Jesus, he makes use of three equivocal terms in the course of his exhortation, so that there are no less than eight theoretically possible interpretations of the passage as a whole: (1) Does *hyparchōn* mean "being originally" or "continuing to be"? (2) Does *harpagmon* mean "something to be clung to" or "something to be striven for"? (3) and above all, does *ekenōsen* mean "evacuated" or "bestowed"? (You can "empty" a jug of its contents or you can "empty" the contents out of the jug.) Thus the passage can be rendered: "When he was in the form of God, he did not look upon this equality with God as something to be clung to, but emptied himself of it and took (instead) the form of a servant." But it can equally well be rendered: "Continuing to be in the form of God, he did not look upon this equality with God as something that needed to be striven for, but he poured himself out on us and took (in addition) the form of a servant." And there are, grammatically at least, a number of other possible renderings lying between these extremes.

Mascall believes that it is right to take the latter rendering, where the primary characteristic of Jesus that the apostle exhorts his brethren to imitate is not his humility but his generosity. Humility comes in indeed, and most impressively, but *after* he had "taken the form of a servant and been born in the likeness of men." It was when he was "found in human form" that he "humbled" himself and became obedient to death, even to death on a cross. And it is in response to his human humility and obedience that God has exalted him in his human nature ("the form of a servant") and has bestowed on him the name that is above every name; so that every knee in creation should bow to him and every tongue confess his lordship as (cf. Isa 45:23) they bow to the name and confess the lordship of God, a name and lordship that in his divine nature ("the form of God") were his already from eternity.

Mascall admits that our human concepts and images are of course inadequate to represent the divine mysteries, but he believes that we are profoundly mistaken, as well as false to the Christian tradition, if we allow ourselves to think of God, in either creation or incarnation, as only able to bestow gifts on creatures by some kind of self-evacuation or self-amputation. That a self-existent and perfect deity should create a world of dependent beings and should then become incarnate in it is rightly seen as overwhelmingly astonishing and unpredictable, but we are mistaken if we try to make it appear more acceptable by giving it a minimizing interpretation. That in Jesus dwells all the fullness of the Godhead bodily (Col 2:9); that in him Godhead is not converted into flesh, but manhood is actually assumed into God; that he is not partly God and partly man or "nearly God" or "as good as God," but one person who is both God and man; and that this does not involve either of the terms being given a reduced or metaphorical sense, but taken quite literally—this, astonishing and unpredictable as it was, can come to be seen by the eye of faith not as less mysterious but as supremely rational.

Generosity, humility and obedience, exaltation, adoration: these, and in that order, are the features of St. Paul's Christology in Philippians. But of kenoticism, as the term is usually understood, the apostle—Mascall submits—cannot be validly accused. And still less of the popular contemporary adoptionism.

The generosity of the suffering Messiah pouring out his life for all in Mark's Gospel (Mark 14:24) expresses the same understanding of the new life that transforms humankind *from* being self-seeking persons *to* becoming self-giving persons *in communion with* their self-giving God. To the extent that any Christian community embodies the suffering Messiah's self-transcending way of the cross, it achieves authenticity, and redemption is furthered in history within the sphere of human life. While the wisdom of the world deems such self-sacrificing love for others foolishness, the converted find in the cross and resurrection of the suffering Messiah the strength to resist that wisdom, and the firm hope and conviction that this self-sacrifice will not prove futile.

Faith in the self-giving God revealed in the self-giving Messiah underpins the dynamism of our charity and hope in the service of divine and human communion (= community or friendship). Such faith implies a universalist view of salvation and authentic human development in every sphere of human life. Theocentric self-transcendence in every sphere of human life is the precondition for human authenticity and community both among all human persons and between them and their God. Christian faith is based on the conviction that a Christocentric life is an authentically theocentric life of self-transcending and self-giving human growth and development. The suffering Messiah represents a revolutionary new notion of divine power as the unrestricted and invincible freedom of self-giving and self-transcending love pouring itself out in the service of all. Christian conversion is our transforming experience of and participation in the divine freedom or power to give ourselves in generously serving others.

3. Diakonia: Conversion as Serving Others

Christ's call to conversion is a call to service (*diakonia*). The Master defines the disciple. The Master came not to be served but to serve and to give his life for all (*kenōsis*). Self-bestowal in the service of

God and others manifests Christian communion *(koinōnia)* with Christ in his giving his life for all. In terms of Pauline theology's concept of Christ as the perfect image of God (2 Cor 3:18–4:4), we see the God who serves all humankind in the service of Christ; and we are transformed or "converted" according to the image of the serving God in the serving Christ.

Conversion, both as an event and a lifelong process, is our communion *(koinōnia)* with the serving God in his serving Christ. Conversion, as event, begins with our first self-giving *(kenōsis)* contribution or help *(diakonia)* to others in the Spirit of the serving Father and Son; it continues as a lifelong process of communion *(koinōnia)* with the community-creating and community-sustaining triune God. The God of Christians is a community *(koinōnia)* of the triune communion whose self-giving *(kenōsis)* serves humankind by transforming us into self-giving and serving persons for the fullness of life in that communion with all others. The triune God's self-giving service is for a universal community *(koinōnia)* without limits.

The God of all is for all, serving all by integrating all in the reciprocity and fullness of divine and human communion *(koinōnia)*. The triune communion is the origin-ground-direction-destiny of all human life, the ultimate origin-ground-direction-destiny of all authentic self-giving service and communion/community/friendship in the event and lifelong process of human conversion (transformation/development/maturation). If the real self is to be fully known in communion with God and all others, we are even now beginning to know our real selves to the extent that in the self-giving Spirit of Christ and his Father we are learning to be generous in the service of others at every level of our lives: intrapersonal, interpersonal, social, national, international. Self-idolatrous thinking and acting precludes, at every level, our coming to know our real selves: *together with* all others under the sovereignty of our self-giving and integrating God.

Having a self to give and actually giving it is at the heart of all communion or personal life, human and divine. *"Diakonia"* means that our self-giving *(kenōsis)* genuinely supports or contributes to others.

4. Koinōnia: Conversion as Friendship, Communion, Community

Conversion is always a call to communion or community or friendship with God and all others: *metanoia* is for *koinōnia* its term. The thought of Aquinas contributes to our appreciation of what all these terms mean in Christian life. Friendship, for Aquinas, is the aim of all human and divine law: ". . . the purpose of the great commandment is charity; since every law aims at establishing friendship, either among human persons, or between them and God, therefore the whole Law is comprised in this one commandment, 'Thou shalt love thy neighbor as thyself,' as expressing the purpose of all commandments" (*S.T. I-II*, q.99, a.1, ad. 2); ". . . the primary aim of human law is to create friendship between man and man" (*S.T. I-II*, q.99, a.2); "Charity is friendship . . . since there is a communication between man and God, inasmuch as He communicates his happiness to us, some kind of friendship must needs be based on this same communication, of which it is written (1 Cor 1:9): 'God is faithful, by Whom you are called unto the friendship of his Son.' The love which is based on this communication is charity: therefore it is clear that charity is the friendship of man for God" (*S.T. I-II*, q.23, a.1); "Charity is a certain friendship of man to God through which man loves God and God loves man; and thus there is effected a certain association of man to God" (*III Sent*. d. 27, q.2, a.1. Cf. *S.T. I-II*, q. 28 a.1); ". . . friendship consists in communication" (*In Eth.* 1658); ". . . mutual love is prescribed to man by divine law" (*III Contra Gentiles* c. 117); ". . . it is impossible to have charity without faith and hope. Charity signifies not only the love of God, but also a certain friendship with Him; which implies, besides love, a certain mutual return of love, together with mutual communion, as stated in *Ethics* viii. This is clear in 1 John 4:16: 'He who abides in charity abides in God, and God in him' and from 1 Cor 1:9 (above). Now this friendship of man with God, which consists in a certain familiar colloquy with Him, is begun here, in this life, by grace, but will be perfect in the future life by glory; and both these things we hold by faith and hope. Therefore just as friendship with a person would be impossible, if one disbelieved in, or despaired of, the possibility of their fellowship or familiar colloquy; so too, friendship with God, which is charity, is impossible without faith, so as to believe in this fellowship and colloquy with God, and to hope to attain this fellowship. Therefore, charity is quite impossible without faith and hope.''

Conclusion

Bernard Lonergan's theology of religious and Christian conversion has implications for a fourfold development in terms of the categories *metanoia, kenōsis, diakonia,* and *koinōnia.* These categories represent four complementary dimensions of religious and Christian conversion both as event and lifelong process. They are employed to explicate the universalist and communitarian dimension of Christian conversion in response to the grace and demand of the God of all whom Jesus Christ as suffering Messiah reveals to be in the service of all in establishing communion, community, and friendship among all and between them and himself. Christian conversion as an event and a lifelong process entails human transformation *(metanoia)* in every sphere of human life. The theocentric self-transcendence of those who adhere to Jesus Christ and his way of costly and generous self-giving *(kenōsis)* service *(diakonia)* is a transforming and integrating participation *(koinōnia)* in the freedom and power of God's pouring out his life for all. Jesus Christ reveals the covenant/community-creating and covenant/community-sustaining God in pouring out his life for all. Christian conversion occurs wherever we are becoming covenant or community persons pouring out our lives in the Spirit of Jesus and his Father for others in every sphere of human life. Christian conversion, represented by Jesus Christ's way of the cross, is a lifelong process of self-transcending love: the only way for the achievement of authentic human development and integration for *all* human persons.

Self-transcendence in conversion is never exclusively for the good of the self, as if the self were not relational to the common good of all. Self-giving must be theocentric; it must be measured by the divine intention for universal communion or community under the sovereignty of the divine truth and goodness which alone enable such community.

CHAPTER FIVE

The Graves of Craving
and the Empty Tomb

The Graves of Craving is the name given to the place where the Israelites literally killed themselves by their gluttonous feeding on the abundance of quail that Yahweh had sent to them during their exodus from Egypt: "The name given to this place was the Graves of Craving, because it was there that they buried the people who had indulged their cravings" (Num 11:34).

The name Graves of Craving is a powerful metaphor for the self-destruction that is consequent upon the "self-fulfillment" that is self-idolatry. Self-gratification, self-indulgence, self-satisfaction, and the abandonment of ourselves to our cravings can become a way of life that is ultimately the way to the death of the spirit that the Old Testament expresses in terms of forgetting God: "But they soon forgot his works: they did not wait for his counsel. But they had a wanton craving in the wilderness and put God to the test in the desert" (Ps. 106:13f).

The Graves of Craving symbolize the destiny of those who do not believe that God will take care of them, who do not trust that he will sustain them: "They tested God in their heart by demanding the food they craved. They spoke against God, saying 'Can God spread a table in the wilderness? He smote the rock so that water gushed out and streams overflowed. Can he also give bread or provide meat for his people?' '' (Ps 78:18-20). The orientation to the Graves of Craving is that of persons who, unable to believe and trust in the sustaining goodness of God, look to themselves for their own self-fulfillment: ''. . . his anger mounted against Israel because they had no faith in God, and did not trust his saving power'' (Ps 78:21-22).

Joseph F. Wimmer links the hunger and temptation of Israel in the desert to that of Jesus (Matt 4:1-11; Luke 4:1-13; Mark 1:12-13).[1] Jesus experiences hunger and is tempted by the devil to satisfy that hunger in his own way. The reply of Jesus to the tempter implies that God alone can satisfy the hunger of the human heart. Pleasure, power, and honors cannot take the place in the human heart that God alone can fill; they must not become idols. Jesus entrusts his life to God's care; he is convinced that God alone can satisfy his hunger and will do so in his own way and time. He rejects, however implicitly, the self-idolatry of self-fulfillment. No human self can fulfill what God alone fulfills. Self-fulfillment is an illusion.

Hunger Is a Reminder

In the desert temptation of both the Israelites and Jesus, the suffering involved in the experience of hunger is not identified as evil; rather, the question of evil arises in terms of how that hunger is to be satisfied. The experience of hunger becomes a symbol for the painful incompleteness of finite human persons longing for fulfillment. Will that hunger of the human spirit ultimately be satisfied on our terms or on God's terms? "Not my will, but thine" (Luke 22:42) is the implicit answer of Jesus and his followers to that question. The religious conscience begins with the awareness that the self is not the central pivot of the universe. The fulfillment of God's will for us, as opposed to that of our own independent self-will, is the condition for the authentic fulfillment of human persons in the resurrection of the just.

Human life, for the religious conscience, is from start to finish gift; and we are responsible to the Giver for the use of that gift. Human authenticity, therefore, can never be taken for granted; it must ever be achieved in the struggle to discern and to fulfill God's will for us. Self-righteousness, like self-sufficiency, is a form of self-idolatry or specious fulfillment. The most severe threats of the Gospel are directed to those who are committed to the illusion of their self-sufficiency:

> But alas for you who are rich: you are having your consolation now.
> Alas for you who have your fill now: you shall go hungry.
> Alas for you who laugh now: you shall mourn and weep.
> Alas for you when the world speaks well of you! This was the way their ancestors treated the false prophets. (Luke 6:24-26).

The hunger of Jesus in the desert recalls the hunger of the Israelites, which God employed for their growth and maturation: ". . . he made you feel hunger . . . to make you understand that man does not live on bread alone but that man lives on everything that comes from the mouth of God" (Deut 8:3). Love is the reason for the hunger of the human heart. God's love is compared to that of a father for his child. He makes his child feel hunger because he wants him to grow and develop into the fullness of that life which he alone can give: "Learn from this that Yahweh your God was training you as a man trains his child" (Deut 8:5). The educational process meets with success to the extent that we learn to love God and what he loves despite the slowness and uncertainty of our growth in following the ways and reverencing him (Deut 8:6).

There is a way of living with the hunger of the human heart which, according to the teaching of Jesus, leads to the deep happiness which he himself experienced: "Happy those who hunger and thirst for what is right: they shall be satisfied" (Matt 5:6). Jesus implies that God loves what is right: Therefore, in our hungering and thirsting for what is right, we mature in loving what God loves and participate more fully and actively in his love. Communion with God is the ultimate beatitude available to humankind. Even now, something of this beatitude is experienced—however imperfectly—by those who hunger and thirst for what is right. Hungering and thirsting for what is right implies communion with God in loving what God loves; it indicates the coming of the kingdom of God, the new order of relationships created by the love for what is right in response to God's gift of his love and its demands for righteousness; it is opposed to the self-righteousness of religious legalism or ideological fanaticism.

God Alone Satisfies

The hunger of the human spirit not only expresses its painful incompleteness and dependence, but also its call to the fulfillment that accrues from seeking and doing what is right. It affects our lives at every level. It pervades our imagination, feelings, interests, thoughts, desires, convictions, decisions, and actions. Hunger expresses our keen awareness of the gap we experience between what we are and what we ought to be, between the real and the ideal at every level of our personal and social experience.

We experience the social dimensions of hunger in those areas where our lives as individuals are relatively fulfilled. A saint may hunger for the companionship of other saints; a theologian, for that of other theologians; an intellectual, for that of other intellectuals; an athlete, for that of other athletes. By the same token, we may least experience hunger in its social dimensions in those areas where our lives are least developed, and where they show the least promise for development.

Where there is hunger there is hope that someone or something may satisfy our hunger. The experience of God's love in religious conversion transforms our experience of such hope by creating a basic consciousness that relativizes all things as gifts from the All, so that the limit of our expectation ceases to be the grave, and our concern reaches beyond the ultimate limits of our world to God, the originating value of every finite good. Religious conversion destroys our idols and lets God be God. Hunger and thirst, in this context, symbolize a radical faith, hope and love: "God, you are my God, I am seeking you, my soul is thirsting for you . . ." (Ps 63:1).

Hunger and thirst symbolize our unsatisfied desires. Vatican II, in its "Pastoral Constitution on the Church in the Modern World," speaks of the basic imbalance rooted in the heart of the human person, where many elements wrestle with one another.[2] Thus, on the one hand, as a creature he experiences his limitations in a multitude of ways. On the other, he feels himself to be boundless in his desires and summoned to a higher life. There is a tendency to look forward to a genuine and total emancipation of humanity wrought solely by human effort, to believe that the future rule of man over the earth will satisfy every desire of his heart.[3] The same pastoral constitution speaks of a prolongation of biological life that is unable to satisfy that desire for a higher life which is inescapably lodged in every human heart. It teaches that man has been created by God for a purpose beyond the reach of earthly misery and bodily death; it affirms that God calls man so that with his entire being he might be joined to him in an endless sharing of a divine life beyond all corruption.[4] Mere man cannot satisfy his boundless desires, his radical hunger and thirst, for a Reality that transcends the finite limits of his own.

To worship one's self or humanity (in self-realization) is a form of idolatry that Otto Baab describes in his study of Old Testament theology:

> Idolatry is well understood in the Bible as differing from the pure worship of Israel's God in the fact of its personification and objectification of the human will in contrast with the superhuman transcendence of the true God. When an idol is worshiped, man is worshiping himself, his desires, his purposes and his will . . . As a consequence of this type of idolatry man was outrageously guilty of giving himself the status of God and of exalting his own will as of supreme worth.[5]

Richard Sennett warns that a society in which liberation of self replaces liberation from the self as an ideal has obliterated any possibilities of self-transcendence from its moral life.[6] Instead of transcending the self, one makes it into a comprehensive standard of reality. One does not, according to Sennett, balance public against private; instead, one assumes that one is, that life is authentic, when one focuses inward, taking moments of self-disclosure in the family to be the ultimate reality in which the self is nourished. The outside is vaguely threatening but also simply vague, a reality of necessities, constraints upon the self, bonds to be broken. It is this intimate imagination, Sennett believes, that destroys the idea of self-transcendence; and when that idea is destroyed, the moral life of society has become fully secularized. Transcendence of the self is at the heart of the Judeo-Christian tradition and its hopes for the regeneration of man in obedience (responsibility) to the grace and demand of the one true God.

Idols Devour

Our belief in transcendence is characterized by the recognition that our impulse life may be destructive as well as constructive, that there is an ambivalence in our spontaneous impulse for self-gratification. Aleksandr Solzhenitsyn implicitly recognizes this problem when he criticizes the view that evil lies only or primarily in society's structures:

> Gradually it was disclosed to me that the line separating good and evil passes not through states, nor between classes, nor between political parties either—but right through every human heart. . . . Since then I have come to understand the truth of all the religious of the world: they struggle with the evil *inside* a human being (inside every human being). It is impossible to expel evil from the world in its entirety, but it is possible to constrict it within each person.
> And since that time I have come to understand the falsehood of all revolutions in history: they destroy only *those carriers* of evil contemporary with them (and also out of haste, to discriminate the carriers of good as well). And they then take to themselves as their heritage the actual evil itself, magnified still more.[7]

Like Moloch, idols devour their children. Narcissistic self-worship discloses its self-destructiveness in the self-righteous illusion that the self—as a mere self—can realize itself and its destiny and that humankind can do likewise. People narcissistically obsessed by the desire to "find themselves" become all-too-willing to abandon each other. Nationalism and racism and the ideology of class-hatred express the same self-destructive narcissism.

Responsibility, fear, and shame, according to Cardinal Newman, remind us that "there is One to whom we are responsible, before whom we are ashamed, whose claims on us we fear."[8] Newman believes that this insight is open only to those who already have undergone religious conversion; it is their perception of transcendence in the moral order. Moral obligation has a transcendent origin: consequently, in the process of realizing his freedom man ventures beyond the limits of immanent self-possession; the norm of his life ceases to be self-will and merely human. He allows himself to be taken beyond himself in his faith-response of religious love to the call of God, the Absolute Value that relativizes every created value and endows it with whatever value it may possess. Faith, according to Bernard Lonergan, has a relative as well as absolute aspect.

It places all other values in the light and the shadow of transcendent value. In the shadow, for transcendent value is supreme and incomparable. In the light, for transcendent value links itself to all other values to transform, magnify, glorify them. Without faith the originating value is man, and the terminal value is the human good man brings about. But in the light of faith, originating value is divine light and love, while terminal value is the whole universe. So the human good becomes absorbed in an all-encompassing good. Where before an account of the human good related men to one another and to nature, now human concern reaches beyond man's world to God and to God's world.[9]

Human authenticity is achieved in self-transcendence; it is not achieved in self-absorption. Cognitive self-transcendence overcomes the temptation to identify what is true with what I like, with my feelings, impressions, and desires. It requires the basic humility of meeting the required conditions for making a particular affirmation or negation. Humility recognizes that the truth of a statement *derives from* the evidence and not from the fact that I say that this is so or not so. Giving an explanation to another person or doing research work are similarly acts of humility which imply that the truth of our statements derives from evidence, from the conditions to be met for making them truthfully.

Moral self-transcendence overcomes the temptation to identify the good with my satisfaction. A twofold identification is involved in this temptation: to identify what satisfies me with my true good and, ultimately, with my Supreme Good. This implies arrogating to myself the attribute of divinity; for only God can identify the objective good and the Supreme Good with what pleases him! In succumbing to this temptation, our world is restricted by egoism. We fail to realize our true possibilities for friendship, benevolence, self-sacrifice, and social responsibility. The self-consumed egotist is a very boring person. Narcissism imprisons him within its narrow confines.

Religious self-transcendence is both an event and a process that overcomes the temptation to idolatry, to make myself or any finite good the supreme value of my life, to restrict my love to what is limited or confined. Loving the Supreme Good that transcends every finite good is transcending myself in the ultimate fulfillment of my capacity for self-transcendence. It is the experience of an unrestricted love without limits or qualifications or conditions or reservations; it liberates us from idolatry, from restricting our love to a limited value or good, from the distortion that follows upon a love that substitutes the relative for the Absolute, the part for the Whole or all-encompassing Good.

The Empty Tomb Reveals

Cognitive, moral, and religious self-transcendence implicitly answer the question: Who is God? I, myself? or Someone to whom I must surrender myself without conditions, qualifications or reservations at every level of my being, a Creator of other persons whose value is equal to mine, the Creator of a marvelous universe that merits my attention, whose laws I must respect with due humility.

The crucified and risen Jesus (and his Church) offers a very exigent norm with respect to divine and human love. Whatever the cost and suffering in self-sacrifice, self-transcending love—the law of the cross—liberates us from the confining prison of self-absorption and our illusions of a merely human fulfillment, a self-fulfillment or self-realization, to be achieved through our purely human resources (ideologies, programs, structures, laws, and so on). God's gift of his love frees us from self-idolatry in its countless forms; it opens a vast and wonderful horizon that inspires us with the ambition of becoming as perfect and generous as our heavenly Father and our crucified Brother.

If the Graves of Craving bear witness to a self-destructive ideal of self-fulfillment, the Empty Tomb of the crucified and risen Jesus tells another story. The Good News of Jesus Christ, proclaimed in the words and deeds of his community of faith, is of a fulfillment that God alone can give.

CHAPTER SIX

The Perilous Project of Communion

Pastoral, tragedy, and melodrama are three literary forms that reflect three distinct interpretations of human life. This essay examines what these literary forms have to tell us about the perilous project of communion.

1. The (American) Pastoral Version of Experience

In his article "American Pastoral" (*Thought* 27/102, 1952, pp. 365–380), John P. Sisk explains how a particular literary form reflects a basic human aspiration and its liabilities. Sisk's examination of the relationship between literature and life in American pastoral is relevant to the human problematic reflected in both the tragic and melodramatic interpretations of human experience. An overview of Sisk's study of American pastoral allows insights to emerge about the interrelationship of these three versions of human experience.

Pastoral poetry idealized shepherds and shepherdesses in idealized rustic surroundings. The pastoral form is artificial and unnatural. However, if we turn from the subject matter conventionally associated with pastoral to the attitude that is at work in this subject matter, we discover that the essential thing in pastoral, according to Sisk, is a certain critical vision of simplicity. It is basically critical because it is an argument. Its argument is that a certain simple state of affairs is more desirable than a certain complex state of affairs. To state its case effectively, it must use the tools of argument, among them abstraction and hyperbole. Abstracting from life only what will not hurt its cause, it too often exaggerates unscrupulously in the interest of the cause. Ironically, then, in the very act of opposing truth to falsehood, what truth the pastoralizer possesses is distorted into falsehood. The only kind of pastoral hero the creator of pastoral is safe with is a sentimentalized abstraction (e.g. the artificial cowboy) who represents no real threat to him and in whom he can pleasantly pretend to believe. Thus the pastoral hero is a safe hero only when he is ridiculously mythified and in general lied about. Then, ironically again, the very act that pretends to be revealing hypocrisy is itself hypocritical.

The pastoral hero is a person in whom innocence, simplicity, and natural insight combine in a remarkable degree. He is clear-visioned, uncomplicated, sure of his aim, close to and in rapport with nature. To the artificial and manufactured he opposes and champions the nature-made or its symbolic equivalent. He lives where the air is pure, close to the great throbbing heart of things. His intercourse with his primal source of power and wisdom is intuitive and mystic rather than discursive and rational. Recalling Rousseau's Noble Savage, he is a free being who draws directly from nature virtues that raise doubts as to the value of civilization. He is, in short, the sort of person that Americans have for generations idealized and flattered themselves that they are, or very nearly are.

American history is markedly pastoral: there is always the wilderness, the prairie, the frontier, the wide-open spaces. There is always the awareness of an older, debilitated, hopelessly artificial and complex civilization, at once watching with awe and being dramatically criticized and found wanting. And when Europe is too distant to offer the opposition needed for complete pastoral, there is the Europeanized Atlantic seaboard, and after that big-city life wherever it may be. American beginnings are endlessly recalled in pastoral stories of a young, hearty, clean-blooded, freedom-seeking, wilderness-encircled band finding a physical and spiritual vigor in its primitive environment and asserting itself boldly and successfully against an effete, oversophisticated fatherland.

The pastoral pattern is established early and grooved deeply. It provides a way of conceiving of oneself dramatically, even mythically, in an environment often malign. It provides a way of cheering oneself up, of compensating for inferiority feelings—for the complex, the effete, and sophisticated continue to inspire the worshiper of the pastoral hero with misgivings. It provides that sense of personal identification with forces beyond the transient and particular and personal, so necessary if one is to go effectively about one's business. In short, it makes poetry (often dangerous) out of the crude materials of living.

Pastoral proper is the offspring of civilization; for the man contending with the wilderness is too busy to adopt a dramatic or pastoral attitude toward himself. The pastoralizer must have leisure and well-being to criticize and idealize. He must have time to realize his dissatisfaction with his nonpastoral condition. The pastoral temper begins to flower in Emerson, Thoreau, and the Transcendentalists, who oppose nature and simplicity to the sterilizing artificialities of industrial civilization. They walk out into the fields on Sunday instead of going to church; they get through directly and intuitively to the true and the real, eschewing the pedestrian intermediaries (an important element in all romantic and most American pastoral); they leave the soul-frustrating, custom-blinded conventions of organized society to find in strange but vital country new power and new insights, which they turn back critically upon society.

The American pastoral impulse expresses itself proteanly in many forms. There is, for instance, the pastoral hero as Indian scout, as trailblazer, as riverboat captain, as cowboy, as Texas Ranger, as backwoodsman. Here it is not the fact of such occupations, but a certain idea about them that counts. The hero is simple, clear-visioned, clean and strong but relatively uncomplicated in mind and passion. He draws his strength from an environment that, if it is not nature, is symbolically equivalent to it. He is a relatively abstract, idealized criticism of organized, artificial, debilitating civilization. Again, the pastoral hero becomes the farmer, the dweller in small villages, the cracker-barrel philosopher, the homespun Socrates: a Scattergood Baines, a Will Rogers, a Davy Crockett. He embodies the belief that true wisdom can come (or can only come) by way of nature rather than nurture; that civilization, particularly big-city civilization, sophisticates and shallows the human soul, whereas plain country-living simplifies and deepens it.

Moving closer to our time, there is the pastoral hero as pilot, as child, as successful boob, as common man, as youth, as social misfit, even as gangster. Again, it is the idea, not the fact, of such figures that expresses the pastoral impulse; for anyone can become the object of worship in the cult of simplicity—anyone who because of period of life or occupation or location can be looked at as having a clarifying, uncomplicated, invigorating contact with what is considered most true, most real, most ultimate. The adolescent (Huckleberry Finn, Orphan Annie) can be looked to for clear-eyed, infallible evaluation—even oracular utterance (man-made civilization has not yet contaminated the pristine innocence of his soul). Youth and beauty can be idealized and mythified, particularly in a materialistic culture terrorized by the fact of mutability, so that movie stars and bathing beauties sound as if they are on the verge of blossoming into full-fledged pastoral heroes with the usual extraordinary insights and alignments with elemental sources of power. In the latter instance nature is passion and the "spiritual" satisfactions of passion-living, which are supposed to be the special province of youth and beauty.

The successful boob is a version of the pastoral hero that has done well in films: Buster Keaton, Laurel and Hardy, Abbott and Costello, Danny Kaye, Martin and Lewis, Bob Hope have exploited this role for all it is worth. In a comic context the boob represents again the triumph of nature over nurture. He objectivizes the common man's desire to succeed without striving and his need to feel that there is in him naturally some precious element that guarantees success without striving. In a cluster of pastoral heroes outside the law—desperadoes, racketeers, gunmen, and philosophic prostitutes—there is the appeal of a direct, even "pure," revolt against organized, complicated, hypocritical, tyrannical civilization (but these may best be called the heroes of crypto-pastoral, since it is difficult to mythify or idealize them too overtly).

For all its surface concern with simplicity, pastoral is really a complex affair whose critical vision of simplicity may be rooted in enlightenment ideas, in nineteenth-century romanticism and humanitarianism, in fascism, in American individualism, or in any combination of these or other ingredients. Its implications are not infrequently anarchist, Marxist, or socialist, for these are directions easily taken when pastoral reacts critically to a particular culture. The pastoralizer idealizes, simplifies, and mythifies values in a work that a certain audience will accept, setting the value-carrying hero in a context that will allow his nature, truth, and simplicity dialectically to assert themselves against a state of affairs that denies these values. The pastoral hero may even (especially if he is in the tradition of the Enlightenment) sound like a champion of reason (as in Marxist pastoral). But even then it will be a "given" natural reason, to which is opposed a "made" sophisticated reason. Generally the American pastoral hero has come by his insight or vision by mainly nonrational means. He possesses wisdom and power not possible to those whose lives are conventional, rational, disciplined, and sophisticated.

All the same, behind the pastoral urge there is, no doubt, a genuine need for a state of complete simplicity: the need to feel whole, justified, in spiritual rapport with the elemental forces of the universe. It manifests whatever it was that drove Descartes to reduce reality to the clear and simple idea, or whatever it is that drives anyone to seek for the master idea or principle that will integrate and explain the bewildering complexity of life.

One chief value of pastoral, whether it expresses itself in art form or is simply a characteristic element in one's habitual attitude toward life, consists in the vision of simplicity that it offers to those who cannot achieve simplicity existentially. It may, depending on its value, point the way to genuine simplicity; it can at any rate offer a symbolic experience of simplicity. Pastoral flourishes wherever the human condition is cramped with complexity and artificiality, wherever it feels itself cut off from the main current of life. The fact that American culture is no longer as simple as it once was explains in part the extensive pastorality of its present attitudes and the number and variety of its pastoral heroes.

Pastoral as expression of the appetite for simplicity is, of course, healthy enough. However, a culture too pressingly in need of pastoral to be very discriminatory or disciplined in its search for it has something wrong with it. The same holds for a culture too sloth-fully in love with complexity, artificiality, and triviality to want any-thing more from pastoral than a comfortable, narcotic daydream. Current American pastoral is generally soft-headed fantasy, sen-timentality, innocuous satire, and adolescent mythification of the past. It has little regard for genuine simplicity and innocence and wants only to toy with the idea of them for the thrill of it. The real problem is that modern Americans pastoralize themselves too read-ily, believing themselves to be firmly in possession of the critical vision of simplicity. The result is the ease with which they accept oversimplified accounts of their own past and the certainty with which they assess the complexity and sophistication of the world they live in, particularly those parts of it they do not immediately live in.

Most American pastoral presumes that simplicity is easily at-tained; that it is an American heritage—given rather than earned. This kind of pastoral has little regard for the simplicity that really matters: that which is earned by mastering complexity. Much Ameri-can pastoral is an escape from complexity, an implicit admission that the conditions of modern life baffle our attempt to find pattern and meaning. Because the vision of simplicity that is retreated to is not really believed in either, there is the implicit admission that pattern and meaning are possible only in fantasy or have, at best, personal rather than general validity. Pastoral can, therefore, be founded on despair. The pastoralizer can confront the despair and pastoralize on it after the fashion of Hemingway or Henry Miller. Both are stoi-cally aware of themselves as embattled heroically with enveloping chaos.

It is dangerous to turn despairingly away from complexity to seek temporary comfort in naive and sentimental fantasies of simplicity. Complexity must be faced and contended with: simplicity must be earned in it. It is dangerous to assume that complexity is all illu-sion, that is can be overcome by turning away from it, or that by sheer force of will simplicity can be imposed on it. Complexity makes easy victims of those who refuse in this way to contend with it.

Hemingway, for example, as pastoral writer of *Across the River and Into the Trees,* can only pastoralize effectively when he has abstracted from life much that cannot be abstracted without seriously distorting it. Correspondingly, the antipastoral world of convention his hero objects to is itself a distortion, created to display to best advantage the virtue and simplicity of that mainly antirational hero whose insight and power stem from his proximity to the throbbing heart of things: Hemingway's nature, found only in the immediate, physical, existential fact of experience. Hemingway's pastoral hero lives life close to the bone, rejecting the inadequacies of a life cluttered up with cerebration and critical idealism and spirituality. This kind of pastoral simplicity is hardly distinguishable from the nihilism that rejects interpretative formulations of experience that assume any objective or real ground of truth.

2. The Tragic Version of Experience

We not only write tragedy and melodrama but also, in quite non-literary contexts, view human experience tragically or melodramatically.

Tragedy is the name not only of a literary form but of an aspect of human life. When we speak of "the tragic sense," we affirm an attribute not only of writers and what they write but of a human being who has a certain way of contemplating experience. Our association between a kind of experience in life and a comparable experience in the imagined life of drama is not arbitrary. The same interpretative vision is operative in both.

Tragedy is a specific form of experience that needs to be differentiated from all other catastrophic disturbances of human life. Aristotle's definition of the tragic hero enables differentiation. The two main terms in his account of the hero are that he is a good man and that he gets into trouble through an error or shortcoming, for which the standard term is "the tragic flaw." The fundamental goodness of the person is jeopardized by an element of inconsistency within his or her character—the potentially self-destructive element that is also, of course, sometimes discernible in social groups: families, communities, nations. Goodness and inconsistency (flawedness) imply conflicting incentives, conflicting needs, and desires. There are pulls and counterpulls within the personality pulling it apart. The integrity (integration or wholeness) of the personality is threatened by "the tragic flaw'' or inconsistency, the disintegrating or dividing element. (The New Testament confronts this problem in terms of the self-destructive futility of trying to serve two masters.) The thinking of the tragic hero is a polyphony, where several thoughts are working simultaneously, one of which is the bearer of the leading voice. The other thoughts represent the medium and low voices, which are not always in harmony with the leading voice but discordant. For his own inner peace the tragic hero must make up his mind and decide in favor of this or that voice.

Tragedy connotes the depth of dividedness or inconsistency within human nature, the belief that we enclose within ourselves certain antinomies or a war of instincts, impulses, and incentives. Antigone, for example, cannot be true to family duty and love without contravening civil law; and Creon cannot maintain civil order without punitive decrees that violate the human sense of justice. Hamlet and Orestes cannot vindicate their fathers, the victims of evil deeds, without themselves committing evil deeds. The tragic hero is pressed to decision by the divisions, pulls, and counterpulls, in life and in himself. There are alternatives competing for the hero's allegiance, and he must select one or the other. Ignorance of alternatives and inability to make decisions cannot produce tragic stature. A degree of mature adulthood is the prerequisite for such stature.

In the tragic view of human experience we are seen in our strength and in our weakness; we experience defeat in victory or victory in defeat; our goodness is intermingled with the power and inclination to do evil; our will is tempered in the suffering that comes with new knowledge and maturity. With its inclusive vision of good and evil, tragedy never sees our excellence divorced from our inclination to love the wrong, nor does it see the evil that we do divorced from our capacity for spiritual recovery.

The tragic view does not treat good and evil as independent wholes or substitute the part for the whole in its complexity. It avoids the reductionism or oversimplification of pastoral. It does not incline toward monopathic attitudes: toward a triumphalism of unqualified hopefulness, a naive optimism that good is chosen without anguish and integrity maintained without precariousness; nor, on the other extreme, toward the despair of our surviving against the villainy of others or of ourselves.

In tragedy the sense of ruin coexists with other elements: impulses and options are dual or multifold and conflicting in their claims to our allegiance. The spectacle of the aged Lear, for example, as victim of madness and the storm, cannot inspire a monopathic pity, for we do not forget that, under the dominion of the dark side of his character, he has created the storm himself. Profound pity for Lear as victim is qualified by our acknowledgment of the paradoxical presence of justice and irony. We experience a concomitant sense of compassion and justice in our recognition of the tragic hero's complexity. (The New Testament affirmations that God alone is good and that Jesus Christ is like us in all but sin express Christian faith in the existence of an absolute divine and human goodness, without limitation, without division or "tragic flaw," a goodness that is normative of all human goodness.)

In tragedy it is assumed that we live simultaneously in two different worlds: the world of desire and the world of limits. There is necessarily a tension between our experience in each of these two worlds that, insofar as we confront it, becomes more explicit as life goes by. We live in the tension of these interacting worlds. Our action is sustained by desire of some kind, by the urge to attain something thought of as good, whatever it may be. Desire pushes against limits in the search for something better. To intervene actively in changing ourselves or our situation we must hold some ideals that differ from our present reality or from our actual situation, so that between the ideal and the reality there prevails a certain tension. Tragedy assumes that human desire can be only partially fulfilled in this life; there always remains a residue of nonfulfillment, of difficulty. Our decision for something better means our imposing limits on ourselves; so desire must come to term with limits. The world of desire is sustained in the world of limits when our plans and ideals succeed in gaining concrete results within that world; otherwise they remain dreams, empty, without substance. In the tragic version of experience life is lived in an area where limits are experienced neither as totally harmonious nor as totally violent; yet limits (e.g. the tragic flaw) are never absent, and the threat of painful experience is never far distant. All deep commitment entails the possibility of experiencing the tragic; for we can fail persons or causes or things about which we care.

In tragedy our liabilities can overtake us, even ruinously. When they do, we are not simply weak, ignorant, cynical, or corrupt because we do not deceive ourselves about our actions. We know our misdeeds and irresponsibility. Tragedy is not so much the truth realized too late, but the way of coming to our senses. We come to understand that we have erred terribly, but we can seek a mode of recovery. In this sense we may say it is our good fortune that tragedy catches up with us; for this can save us from irreparable disaster. Tragedy is the idiom of an imperfect humanity that remains capable of redemption. Although failure is possible, it is not mistaken for the final blow, the road to nothing. Tragedy affirms the hope for self-transcendence (e.g. Peter's repentance after his betrayal of Christ).

In tragedy there is the tension between "I ought" and "I want," between limits and desire, between obligations and passions. Hubris, a traditional constituent of tragic experience, ordinarily implies our self-glorifying aggressiveness, our reckless defiance of the limits entailed in our fundamental commitments, responsibilities, and moral obligations. It deals with our self-destructive temptation to become our own little gods, to reject limiting moral imperatives, to transgress the boundaries of responsible decision and action—persons who refuse to accept these limits are the constant theme of classical tragedy: Oedipus, Macbeth, Dr. Faustus, Phèdre. All know what these limits are, and all of them in the exuberance of passion violate them. Their tragic experience of wrong choices and their consequences results in a humbling self-knowledge. In this respect, the tragic is not disastrous and tragedy is not the dramatic embodiment of despair. There is no tragedy without the affirmation of human dignity and value. Tragic suffering is the matrix for coming to a recognition of our true dignity, one which is always within limits. There is a process within the tragic form of human experience that begins with a *purpose* (to do something about the Theban plague; vindicate the killing of the former king), that moves through *passion* (action, conflict, suffering) and then is followed by *perception* (the wisdom begotten of pursuing the purpose passionately).

The process is similar to that of the artist who thrashes around in the midst of unshaped, impressionistic experience, and then seeks to *express* it, and only then *fully* recognizes what it is that he experienced.

3. The Melodramatic Version of Experience

In tragedy, conflict is inner; in melodrama it is outer. Melodrama dichotomizes human life with division between the good and the evil, the weak and the strong, victors and victims, the human and the inhuman. Melodrama is a way of interpreting human life as a kind of war between angels and devils: a demonology. In melodrama, one attacks or is attacked. Its heroes and villains do not experience inner tensions or struggles. Its heroes are incapable of doing wrong; its villains are incapable of doing good. Heroes attack or are attacked because they are good. Villains attack or are attacked because they are evil. Both heroes and villains enjoy a melodramatic oneness, a singleness of passion or conviction that expresses itself in conflict with whatever stands in its way. The heroes of melodrama are pitted against a force outside of themselves: a specific enemy, a hostile group, a social movement.

The experience of melodrama is monopathic. There is a oneness of feeling in persons who are always undivided, unperplexed by alternatives, untorn by divergent impulses. All their strength or weakness faces in one direction. The competitors or crusaders or aggressors or defenders in melodrama do not experience the mixed feelings of their counterparts in tragedy, which is polypathic. In melodrama we are simply triumphant, hopeless, challenging, defensive, joyful, bitter, purposeful, or victimized. The monopathic melodramatic experience is exhilarating, sensational, and thrilling with little regard for convincing motivation. Melodrama constantly appeals to the emotions. It aims at keeping us thrilled by the awakening, no matter how, of intense feelings of pity, or horror or joy, whereas the complex motivation of tragedy evokes mixed feelings—it is as troubling and burdensome as gaining true self-knowledge must be.

In melodrama we are seen in our strength or in our weakness; in tragedy, both in our strength and in our weakness. In melodrama we are victorious or we are defeated; in tragedy we experience defeat in victory or victory in defeat. In melodrama we are good or evil; in tragedy our goodness coexists with our inclination to evil. In melodrama our will is broken or it conquers; in tragedy it is tempered in the suffering that accompanies personal maturation in the acquisition of new wisdom. Melodrama, in separating good and evil and in treating them as independent wholes, tends toward a belief that human transformation for better or for worse is impossible. Melodrama is the idiom of presumption and despair, of self-righteousness and futility. The Christian message of salvation is meaningless in the melodramatic world, where the good (heroes) have no need of it and the bad (villains) are beyond it. Reconciliation and forgiveness have no place in the melodramatic version of the human condition. Polarization over irreconcilable differences is at the heart of our melodramatic experience.

Heroes in melodrama are not beset by conflicting impulses and values that make decision difficult. They are not accountable for the way in which they handle themselves in those conflicts that make the tragic hero possible; they are efficient and self-assured insofar as they are not reflective. They are naturally single-minded in their decision-making and action.

Elements of competition and rivalry belong to the world of melodrama, to the extent that they focus on the struggle between rather than within people. Ordinarily this is low-key enough not to have melodramatic intensity. There is such ritual heightening in many kinds of athletic competitions that we have the tendency to call them spectaculars and to translate the opposing players into heroes and villains. We have the same tendency in politics, where all combatants turn their campaigns into forays of good against evil, and where much depends on the histrionic devices by which a contestant can excite audiences into uncritical partisanship. On one political side are all the energies of a particular reform; on the other those who equate it with subversion or wrongheadedness.

The spirit of melodrama thrives where rationality is decried and violence is extolled. Revenge and war are basic forms of melodramatic action. As long as we can discern evil in other individuals or groups or institutions, we will have the grounds for melodramatic action both in life and on the stage. Only when we are troubled by the evil that originates within ourselves or our own groups or institutions will we have grounds for tragic action.

Melodrama appeals to our impulse to idealize ourselves and to feel threatened by what is foreign. Foreigners, as well as people of different races or cultures or religious lend themselves to the realm of melodrama. The Chinese spoke of "foreign devils," and other cultures have shared similar sentiments about foreigners. Whatever seems to threaten our values and status quo contributes to the sense of the enemy that is at the heart of melodrama. Gothic novels of eighteenth-century England, for example, were filled with Italian "devils," who melodramatically symbolized the evils most diametrically opposed to cherished English values. Nazi propaganda depicted a pure and innocent Aryan people as victimized by its "foreign devils." Marxist melodrama, with its class warfare, finds its devils in bosses, landlords, capitalists, and the middle class. Blaming classes of people for all the ills afflicting society is melodrama's way of naming the devil for exorcism.

Some Theological Reflections

Pastoral, tragedy, and melodrama reflect our longing for the simplicity and harmony and peace that result from our mastery of both internal and external conflicts. Our pastoral longings are challenged by both our internal inconsistencies and our external conflicts. Our longings are felt at every level: intrapersonal, interpersonal, social, national, and international. The liabilities that we experience in our attempts to satisfy our longings and resolve our conflicts must be critically examined both in real life and its expression in literature and drama.

Our literary forms express our ways of interpreting our experience. They imply that we have achieved the maturity to appropriate our life stories; for this is impossible without forms or modes for interpreting them. Wherever human life stories are being effectively communicated, some literary form or other is, at least implicitly, operative. The gospel, for example, is the literary form the evangelists employed to tell the story of Jesus. The literary form no less than the content of the gospels reflects the cognitive and affective life of the evangelist at every level. The gospel as literature reflects life and serves as a matrix for theological reflection. Our biblical narratives, no less than our living tradition—our history—as the people of God, have a form and content that constitute the foundational matrix for our theological reflection and self-understanding at every level. Our lives of faith and love are expressed in the form and content of both our narratives and tradition.

Our desire for peace has pastoral, tragic, and melodramatic dimensions. Let us clarify this statement. Peace is a question of personal interiority, arising from a right relationship with God. It is also the time when all tears will be wiped away, the time of the eternal banquet in justice and righteousness. Our eschatological vision of peace is that of a reality to be brought about in God's time, by God's action in the completion of human history. Our vision is also a horizon against which we measure the brokenness of the present, and perhaps bring to that brokenness a measure of healing. Peace is also the tranquillity of order in freedom, charity, justice, and truth—a this-worldly possibility whose realization is not an option, but a moral imperative. Catholic incarnational humanism expresses the pastoral longing for peace, but sees human beings as they are: fallen and weak, but still the images of God in history. It has the tragic awareness that the demons within us make conflict inevitable; still, conflict need not lead to mass violence if a rightly ordered peace of political community has been established. The better angels of our nature create political communities where conflict can be resolved through law and governance. There is no ineluctable slippery slope from conflict to the melodrama of war. But peace does not simply happen; it must be achieved. The pastoral aspiration is realized by active, committed, and intelligent peacemakers. Christ's way of the cross is that of the Peacemaker both reconciling and integrating all humankind under the sovereignty of God's love and wisdom. The Good Shepherd is the Pastoral Hero giving his life that all humankind might live in the freedom, charity, justice, and truth of his peace. He is effectively leading or governing his people when the Church is actively at the service of peace as a religious community with a distinctive view of the human prospect.

The Church most powerfully addresses the possibilities of the human condition when its anthropology is intimately linked to its Christology. Christ is not only a revelation of God and his saving will for all humankind through the Church but also a revelation of the human person, of what that person was intended to be at creation and is by reason of the incarnation of the Son of God and by reason of the crucifixion, resurrection, and ascension. The Redeemer of the world is the Pastoral Hero in whom the goodness of creation (Gen 1, *passim*) is revealed in a new and more wonderful way. That goodness has its sources in Wisdom and Love. Through sin that creation "was subjected to futility" (Rom 8:20); in Christ it recovers its original link with the divine Wisdom and Love. The Redeemer reconciles and reintegrates the world in the peace and communion that he enjoys with his Father and all humankind. According to Paul (Eph 2:13-18), "[Christ] . . . is the peace between us [Jews and Gentiles], and has made the two into one and broken down the barriers that used to keep them apart, actually destroying in his person the hostility . . . to create one single new man in himself out of the two of them and by restoring peace . . . to unite them both in a single body and reconcile them with God. In his own person . . . he came to bring the good news of peace, peace to you who were far away and peace to those who were near at hand. Through him, both of us have in the one Spirit our way to come to the Father." This peace, which happens in Christ, is communion—of God with humankind and of humans among themselves. This peace does not cease when the earthly ministry of Jesus ceases. Rather, in the Holy Spirit he has given to us a lasting way to the Father. Not only is Jesus "the Way, the Truth and the Life" (John 14:6); so is the Church (e.g. Acts 24:14). This passage from Ephesians locates ecclesial communion (peace) in the triune communion. He is, in fact, the communion (peace) that he gives. He is the Pastoral Hero who overcomes our tragic condition of inner division (inconsistency) and our melodramatic condition of external conflicts and war by sharing the peace of his triune communion for the transforming integration of all human life.

Biblical eschatological banquet symbolism expresses the pastoral longing of the community of faith for a peace that God alone can give at every level of human life to overcome both the tragic and melodramatic evils besetting us. God will prepare this banquet for all (Isa 25:6; 65:13). The hungry and poor will participate (Isa 55:1). The banquet symbolism entails a melodramatic element of divine judgment: the person without a wedding garment is thrown out into the dark, "where there will be weeping and grinding of teeth" (Matt 22:11-13). The same melodramatic separation of the good and the evil appears in Matthew's account of the Last Judgment (25:31-46) and where Jesus speaks of hell in other Gospel narratives (e.g. Matt 13:42; Mark 9:43-48). The peace of the banquet community is not achieved without a struggle against evils that afflict human life at every level. God is always the ultimate hope for victory in this struggle for peace, and Israel believes that God will send his Messiah for that purpose. When he believes himself certain of victory, the "prince of this world," or Satan, is vanquished in his struggle of cosmic dimensions with Christ (John 12:31; Rev 12:9-13).

There is a melodramatic quality to the conflict between the forces of good and evil, between Christ (Messiah) and Satan. Christ has come to "reduce to impotence him who held the rule of death, the devil" (Heb 2:14). God has sent Christ to "destroy his works" (1 John 3:8). The gospels depict Jesus' public life as a struggle against Satan, the "sons of the devil" (John 8:44), the "brood of vipers" (Matt 3:7). If the resurrection of Christ marks the defeat of Satan, the struggle will only be concluded, according to Paul, with the last act of the history of salvation on the "day of the Lord," when "the Son, having reduced to impotence every principality and every power and death itself, will render the kingdom to his Father, in order that God may be all in all" (1 Cor 15:24-28). We are called to choose between God and Satan, between Christ and Belial (2 Cor 6:14), between the "evil one" and the "true one" (1 John 5:18). On the last day, we shall be forever with one or the other in a state of blessedness or perdition.

Salvation history is expressed melodramatically because it is experienced melodramatically. There is a melodramatic finality to the all-or-nothing state of human fulfillment or self-destruction, of love or unlove. The melodramatic version of human experience is most expressive of our present sense of an ending, our eschatological "not-yet-but-even-now" sense of where our decisions and actions are taking us in the drama of salvation or perdition. The melodramatic version implies that our tragic version of human life best expresses our experience of what is temporary or as yet unresolved in our inner conflicts, inconsistencies, or state of dividedness; and that state will ultimately be resolved forever. Narratives of the healings and exorcisms of Jesus, of his forgiving and reconciling sinners, of his teaching and encouraging—all imply our experience of a graced liberation from the worst possible effects of our "tragic flaws" and our ultimate hope to enjoy the fullness of that liberation with all others in the peace of our Pastoral Hero, his Father, and Spirit.

Divine revelation occurs within the realm of our human experience. That experience has pastoral, tragic, and melodramatic dimensions that constitute the context of divine revelation within the Judeo-Christian tradition. The sacred writings of this tradition contain those three dimensions and reflect thereby the experience of covenant faith. Our critical study of the pastoral, tragic, and melodramatic triptych of human experience can lead to a deeper grasp of revelation, the sacred writings, redemption, and our life in the community of Christian faith. Christ illuminates and transforms all the dimensions of our historical experience.[1] The literary forms of pastoral, tragedy, and melodrama reflect a triptych of human experience that have their unity in the cognitive and affective dynamic of both the individual and society.

In the mystery of the Incarnate Word the mystery of human experience takes on a new light. Christ, the new Adam, the Pastoral Hero of a new people, in the very revelation of the mystery of the Father and his love, fully reveals us to ourselves and brings to light within our historical versions of experience our most high calling. Through the Incarnation God gives human life the dimension he intended it to have from the beginning, delivering us from the ultimate consequences of the tragic flaws that jeopardize the basic goodness of every unit of human society—family, group, community, nation—to integrate us within the kingdom ruled by his peace. Our crucified and risen Savior reveals that our attempts at the "quick fix" for the attainment of human happiness are ultimately self-destructive evasions of the way of the cross, the only way of entry into the peace that God alone can give.

CHAPTER SEVEN

The Good News for Communion

Wittgenstein affirmed that if we claim to know something and cannot give a single example of it, perhaps we do not know what we are talking about. The Church knows what it means by "love"; it points to the Good News that is Jesus Christ, and proclaims that "God is love." We tell the story of Jesus Christ and his people to explain what we mean by "love," human and divine. We judge the goodness of our lives in the light of that love, mindful of the warning that our love "is not to be just words or mere talk, but something real" (1 John 3:18). Jesus' living and dying and rising in God's love measures the reality of our love for God and neighbor. If the Great Commandment is a question of loving God above all and our neighbor as ourselves, the four Gospels are the Church's answer to what that loving means.

From the start, the Church has felt the need for all four Gospels as normative or canonical for ascertaining Christian authenticity. The Diatessaron, the edition of the four Gospels in a continuous narrative, compiled by Tatian about 150 to 160, had widely circulated from an early date in the Syrian-speaking Church, where it became the standard text of the Gospels down to the fifth century, when it gave way to the four separate Gospels. The experiment of the Syrian Church had failed. The Diatessaron was no adequate substitute for the four distinct Gospels and their complementary theologies as the New Testament community's norm for ascertaining and promoting

Christian authenticity. Mark was not enough; rather, four distinctive theologies, or ways of telling the Good News, were not only required to serve as the norm for Christian authenticity, but they also sufficed.

Significantly, the four Gospels were written over a period of time that would correspond to the average person's life span and phases of development and maturation at the intrapersonal, interpersonal, and social levels. The developmental challenges that faced the first generation of Christians are the same in both essence and structure that face it in every subsequent generation; hence, the canonicity or normative value of the four Gospels, which correspond to four phases of challenge and response both for the attainment of Christian adulthood and for ascertaining Christian authenticity.

The Gospels serve as the Church's fourfold norm for discerning whether we are living in God's love, or "knowing" God in the biblical sense of intimacy and friendship. The Church employs its Gospels in its pedagogy for Christian conversion both as event and lifelong process, recognizing that such conversion is grounded on the grace and demand of God's love in Jesus Christ. The New Testament imperatives to watch and pray always remind us that conversion is a precarious process in which we risk falling into temptation. Hearts grow cold. The New Testament tells of those who have fallen in love with God in Christ and who have later fallen out of love. There is no moment when Christians, as individuals and as a community, may comfortably assume there is no longer any need to watch and pray lest they fall into temptation.

The Gospels represent four complementary aspects of the Christian community's authentic response to God's gift of his love in Jesus Christ and his Spirit. The Gospel of Mark summons us to the costly commitment of the way of the cross: "If any man would come after me, let him deny himself and take up his cross and follow me. For whoever loses his life for my sake and the gospel's will save it" (8:34f). Mark's stress on service for the good of all (10:43 and 14:24) is linked to total self-giving to God (15:34); for only when we totally surrender ourselves to God are we free to serve others without using them for our own self-interest. Letting God be God is the only basis for a well-ordered love of ourselves and all others in fulfillment of the Great Commandment. Mark sees in the suffering Messiah the face of a loving God serving all humankind, giving his life for all without counting the cost. The self-abandonment of the crucified is the self-gift of God for all. The suffering Messiah reveals the divine power as self-giving love rather than as merely miracle-working or that "quick-fix." True love means costly commitment to God in his service of all. Our lives are shaped by our freely chosen commitments and the persons, divine and human, to whom we have chosen to be responsible. Accepting responsibility before God for ourselves and our neighbor evidences true covenant love and maturity in the spiritual pedagogy of the Judeo-Christian tradition.

The Gospel of Matthew, the Gospel of the Church, stresses the family responsibilities of true love. Accepting Jesus means accepting the whole Jesus: his brothers and sisters, no less than his Father and Spirit. Matthew summons us to life in the family of Jesus, the risen and exalted Son of God who presides over and resides in his Church (28:19-20 and 1:23; 18:20). Jesus declares that his disciples are his true relatives (12:49) and his "brothers" (28:10), and tells the disciples that they, too, are all "brothers" (23:8; also 18:21, 35). Matthew has Jesus stress at once his uniqueness in comparison with his disciples and his relatedness to them: "For whoever does the will of *my Father* in heaven is *my brother, and sister, and mother*" (12:50).

Matthew's Gospel starts with a genealogy. Jesus is depicted as the member of a people. Just as there is no Messiah without his people, so there is no Jesus present in history apart from his Church. Matthew portrays Jesus as a new Moses forming his people into a new Israel. The wealth of precepts and rules for Christian conduct that characterize this Gospel express the demands of an authentic communion with God in the community of Christ's body. Matthew provides a standard for determining the degree of authentic participation in the fellowship-creating reality of the messianic community: to have brought forth the fruits of the kingdom (21:43), to have done the will of God (5:16; 7:21), to have attained to the higher righteousness (5:20), to have shaped one's life course so as to enter into the kingdom by the narrow gate (7:13), to do good works that glorify our heavenly Father (5:16). Matthew's Gospel teaches us that Christ is Emmanuel, God-with-us, the Messiah Son of God in whom God is present among his people, the Church (1:23). God abides with his people in the person of Jesus, who is acting in their fellowship: "Behold, I (the risen Son of God) am with you always, even to the close of the age" (28:20). Matthew edifies (builds up) the first moment of conversion into the second moment, where our turning to God is strengthened by the common bonds of fellowship. Having broken the chains that bind us into ourself, Christ leads us to the new experience of making relationships with him through our relationships with others. If God is love, Matthew sees his face in the brothers and sisters of Christ.

Luke's Gospel stresses the outgoing and universal compassion of God in Jesus Christ's concern for outcasts, sinners, and Samaritans. We have accepted God's gift of his love only when we share his universal compassion for all. The Church's universal mission of evangelization expresses the all-embracing and boundless love of God, which Luke especially underscores in his Acts of the Apostles, the companion volume to his Gospel. The family that works, works for all. The vitality of the Church as the family of Christ will be reflected in its contribution to the world outside it. Evangelization, rather than tribalistic exclusiveness, manifests the vitality of the Church as the body of the universally compassionate Christ. Luke is written for Christians who already adhere to Jesus Christ and his community and who are now seeking to grasp the meaning of this faith commitment and to express it to the world that lies outside the confines of their faith. Persecution has made the Christian community aware of its impact upon the world; it has also created a need for the community to defend and explain itself. To explain oneself to others, one must first be able to understand oneself; one must be able to tell one's own story. The author of Luke-Acts, therefore, explains the roots of the Christian community in the Jewish world and relates the salvation promised to Israel to the entire world.

The plan of Luke-Acts is hinged around the commission of the risen Christ to his disciples: "You will be my witnesses not only in Jerusalem but throughout Judea and Samaria, and indeed to the ends of the earth" (Acts 1:8). At the end of Matthew the risen Christ promises to be with his disciples (28:20); at the beginning of Acts Christ calls his disciples to be with him. In Matthew's Gospel he promises to be where they are: to be with them in their community. At the beginning of Acts he calls them forth to be with him on his missionary journey. Luke's writings represent the maturing Christian's response to the challenge of the world: to the questions, crises, and culture of the times. Christian maturation demands the courage and intelligence to confront the social, political, cultural, economic, and religious complexities of the times. Luke sees the face of God in the universal outreach and compassion of the body of Christ: divine love is love without limits.

John's Gospel locates the unifying principle that underlies the complexity of the three previous phases of Christian development in the gift of the Father's love we receive through the Son and in the Holy Spirit. Christian faith consists in the reception or welcoming of this gift: whoever possesses it begins to love as Christ has loved us. Consequently, love is the only law. John's Gospel synthesizes the entire Christian experience in terms of God's self-gift in Jesus Christ and his Spirit. The Church's confessions of faith, Eucharist, fellowship, Gospels, prayers, precepts, proclamation, rites, service, and witness are called into existence and sustained by the gift of this love that alone constitutes their true meaning and value. Our self-transcending love for God and his Church and his world is a sharing in that of the Blessed Trinity, the community of the three Persons, dwelling within us, encompassing our intrapersonal and interpersonal and social life, as its origin and motive and momentum and goal.

John's Gospel tells us that our outgoing and universal compassion derives from the mutual indwelling of the Father and Son whose Spirit is the life of the Church. Jesus Christ extends his life in the triune communion to all who will welcome it. Just as Jesus dwells in the Father, so his friends dwell in him: "As the Father has loved me, so have I loved you; abide in my love" (15:9).

Eternal life is eternal love with all others in the triune communion, the source and motive and momentum for our free and costly commitment to God, to the Church, and to the world. The self-giving of the Father and Son is manifest in the work of their Spirit bringing forth the fruits of the kingdom (Matt 21:43) that glorify the Father (Matt 5:16) in the messianic community's service of all humankind. John sees in the reciprocal love of Christians both the indwelling and outgoing love of the three Persons as the origin and ground and destiny of all humankind. The Church is the sacrament of the triune communion, the efficacious sign of the eternal friendship/love even now transforming human relationships into relationships of a friendship that not even death itself can terminate. The joy of that friendship is one that this world cannot take from us because it is not this world's to give. John's Good News is that the eternal friendship/love is both God and his will/destiny for us. The divine will for us is always the divine love for us.

The four Gospels are the Christian community's answer to the question, "What is love?" The answer is not an abstract definition, but the concrete story of Jesus living and dying and rising among and for us in God's love. He is the Good News that God is love and loves everyone. We exist because God loves us. The song title "You're Nobody Till Somebody Loves You" captures the Hebrew notion of their having been a nonpeople until God's covenant-creating love called them into existence. The divine will is always the divine love calling us into existence for our development and fulfillment within the triune communion with all others. The Church celebrates that community-creating love as the new life that God has poured out for all in the blood of the new covenant (Mark 14:24; Matt 26:28; Luke 22:20). It knows that love as the Spirit of God which is poured both into our hearts (Rom 5:5) and out upon all humankind (Acts 10:45). The Gospel writers want their hearers to be transformed by the gift and demand of this love at every level of their being: intrapersonal, interpersonal, social, national, and international. Their Good News is that there is available to all the gift of a life and a love that infinitely transcends any merely human life and love: the transcendent love and eternal life of the triune God.

The Gospel truth about the divine love is no abstract attribute but a personal self-disclosure, a divine and beloved Son (John 3:16). And we in turn are called to love God with obedience and fidelity. Pauline and Johannine theology insist on the interpersonal relationship by which we are in Christ and Christ is in us. John presents Jesus as the Father's beloved Son sent into the world as the revelation of God's love (3:16), a love which is at the heart of Christian discipleship, and which grounds the new commandment (13:34), the practical test of the first and greatest commandment. An authentically Christocentric life is the guarantee of a truly theocentric life (the implication especially stressed in Mark's Gospel). Similarly, an authentic commitment to the body of Christ is the guarantee of a truly Christocentric life (the implication of Matthew). Finally, evangelization as an apostolic mission in which we reach out to those who have not heard the Good News is the evidence of a truly pneumatological life in the outpouring of the Spirit of the Father and Son for all. (The implication of Luke, often called the Gospel of the Spirit.) *Nemo dat quod non habet.*

Evangelization is evidence of life in the triune communion; for only those who have the Spirit of the self-giving Father and Son communicate it. Evangelization is the hallmark of authentically theocentric and Christocentric living and loving. The self-giving Father and the self-giving Son are known in the biblical sense of John's Gospel among those who live and love in their Spirit. Evangelization manifests life and love in their self-giving for all. The Spirit is where it acts; and when it acts, it is always self-giving life and love for all.

The Good News is the love that Jesus Christ is and reveals. That love wills the good of others; it acts and works for their welfare. (We perversely tend to imagine that we, as opposed to God, really know what is best for ourselves.) To a lawyer who questions him about inheriting eternal life, Jesus tells the parable of the Good Samaritan and twice insists on the activity of love in the service of God and neighbor: "*Do* this and you will live. . . . Go and do likewise" (Luke 10:28, 37). Paul uses fifteen verbs to present the active ways in which love expresses itself (1 Cor 13:4-7). If this famous hymn of Paul to love in 1 Cor 13 is read by changing the tense of the verbs and substituting the proper name "Jesus" for "love," the passage becomes a description of what Jesus is remembered to have been during his life on earth. It was Jesus preeminently who was remembered to have been patient, kind, not jealous or boastful, arrogant or rude. It was Jesus the servant who did not insist on his own way and was not irritable or resentful; who did not rejoice at wrong but rejoiced in the right. Paul remembers Jesus as the Son of God "who loved me and gave himself for me" (Gal 2:20). He recalls the selfless love of Jesus, who in his concern for others "did not please himself" (Rom 15:3). In Philippians 2:5-11 Paul holds up a verbal icon or image of the character of Jesus as a model for Christian life: the one who humbled himself and took the form of a loving servant and became obedient unto death. He exhorts us to have the same love and to "look not to our own interests, but those of others" (vv. 1-4).

John insists that love must show itself in *action* (1 John 3:18). The love of neighbor is indeed the service of God; for the neighbor is the object of God's creative, sustaining, and redemptive love. Our living activity on behalf of our neighbor expresses our cooperation and collaboration with God's own active love for that neighbor. Our active service of God and neighbor will inevitably be costly; for we are not genuinely committed to persons for whom we are unwilling to suffer. We cannot suffer out of love for others when we have no love for them. The cross represents the costly commitment of all authentically divine and human love. Jesus voluntarily accepts suffering and death out of love for his Father and for all human persons. His acceptance is not passive; rather, it is the supreme activity of divine and human love for all others. In the death and resurrection of Jesus Christ, the Father-love showed itself supremely active in working for the ultimate welfare and highest good of all humankind.

In the Judeo-Christian tradition God is the source and standard of loving. Our loving derives from God's loving and is measured by its standard (1 John 4ff.; Matt 5:48). The divine initiative in loving takes the original and radical form of creating us as loving, inviting, and enabling us to love God in return and persisting with this offer and empowerment despite continuing human refusal. God's love bestows value in bestowing existence, the dignity of being loved by God in the face of failure, and the capacity to return love. Jesus taught that God commands us to love him (Matt 22:37); he demands that same love for himself (John 15:9-10). We know that

God loves us because he has made us response-able. Love given is to be reciprocated in our responsibility to God. The demand for prayer is a summons to responsibility at the intrapersonal and interpersonal or social levels.

The corporate character of Christian prayer expresses the co-responsibility of the new covenant community in the presence of "our" Father. God's persistent love of his covenant people evokes their corporate response in prayerful co-responsibility. The God to whom Christians pray is a community of Persons whose eternal life is one of reciprocal love. Their freely assuming co-responsibility for us is acknowledged and reciprocated in the co-responsible prayer of the Christian community. The Father sends his Beloved Son and the Spirit of their self-giving love for the salvation and integration of all humankind. The corporate prayer or co-responsibility of the Christian community expresses its welcoming acceptance of the Father, his Beloved Son, and their Spirit of love. The liturgical prayer life of the Church is the matrix for its understanding of authentically human and divine love. The love that is revealed in Jesus Christ and the gift of his Spirit find expression in the sacred liturgy of the Church. "Eucharist" means "thanksgiving" for God's self-giving in his Son and Spirit, transfiguring and integrating our lives within the triune communion.

The preaching and teaching of the Church is both a response to and an expression of the meaning of God's gift and demand of love. The Church proclaims and manifests the meaning and goodness of divine and human love, a meaning and goodness that is often violently rejected by the secular world for whom the folly of the cross (1 Cor 1:21, 23) is by no means, as for St. Augustine, the folly of God's love.

The four Gospels are written to serve the purpose of grace and the demand of God's transcendent love in Jesus Christ and his Church. They articulate and objectify the true meaning and goodness and demands of this love for us, both as individuals and as a community. The Church, by telling us the story of Jesus in its Gospels, summons us to put on his mind and heart in order that we may become what God intends us to be within the universal story of his unfolding love. The authenticity of our response to Jesus' injunction to love God above all else finds its measure in the needs by which we follow his way of self-investing love for our neighbor in self-surrender to the Father's universal salvific will for all humankind. The glory of the Father is the brotherhood and sisterhood of all human persons in his Son Jesus Christ. The Father's love for us is the source of our response-ability with regard both to the absolutely Other (God) and to all others. What we have to give is God's love. Our receptivity is the ground of our productivity in sharing Christ's life of service, his shaping of the future into the form of the kingdom of God. The greatest in the kingdom, therefore, is the one most dependent upon and responsive to the Father's love (cf. Matt 18:1-7, 10): Jesus Christ, the Son of God, whose receptivity and response-ability make the fellowship-creating mystery of the Father's love available to all humankind.

The self-transcending love of the Father and Son is eternal life/love in the kingdom of God. It is manifest in the suffering Messiah's service of all humankind in his total self-abandonment to God (Mark), in service of one another in the community of the suffering Messiah (Matthew), and in the service of all humankind (Luke-Acts). The Christian is called to mature in this love by following Jesus in his Church for his world. Mark underscores the Christological dimension; Matthew, the ecclesial; Luke-Acts, the universal; and John, the mystical, that is, the Trinitarian, interpersonal, mutual indwelling of the divine Persons one within the others and with us.

The Father is self-transcending, self-investing love for the Son. The Son is self-transcending, self-investing love of God in their gift to humankind of the one Spirit who binds them and us in mutual, self-fulfilling love within the triune communion. We share in that love by transcending and investing ourselves in following Jesus. We participate in the love by the gift of God's Spirit. We come to fulfillment in that love of the triune communion by our self-abandonment to the Father, by our sharing in his unrestricted love for our fellow members of Christ's Body, and by our sharing in God's outpouring of his Spirit to all humankind. Jesus' way of the cross reveals and communicates the divine self-giving love that liberates us from our self-destructive tendency to self-idolatry at three levels: as individuals attempting to be our own little gods (Mark and Matthew);

as groups succumbing to sectarianism and tribalistic exclusivism (Luke-Acts); as a world community assuming a self-sufficiency without God and hostile to God, the "Johannine world" (John). The self-transcending love that proceeds from God delivers us from alienation at each level for integration and self-fulfillment within the kingdom of God. Only under the sovereignty of God's love can we recognize and accept one another as we truly are: *together with all others* in the triune communion.

In Trinitarian terms, Mark is the Gospel of the mysterious and invisible Father whose love demands our total self-abandonment with Jesus for the coming of his kingdom. Matthew is the Gospel of the Son, of the body of Christ, enabling us to live according to the exigencies of God's self-investing love within the Church. Luke, the Gospel of the Spirit, together with Acts, bears witness to the world of God's universal salvific will/love. John is the Gospel of the indwelling Trinity whose self-transcending love is seen to be the origin and ground and destiny of the Jesus story, the Church story, and the story of the world. Communion with the triune God implies a participation in the dynamic of the divine self-investing love. The Gospels symbolize the unrestricted nature of the triune God's love to which all humankind is constitutively oriented by presenting Jesus as God's self-revelation. They summon us to follow Jesus in his fundamental self-others-world-mystery relationship for the authentic fulfillment of our life story.

The mystery of God's love for us in Jesus Christ generates the faith, hope, and love at the heart of Christian conversion, both an event and a lifelong process. Such conversion means faith in the reality of God's love for us revealed in Jesus Christ. Although the wisdom of the world deems the self-sacrificing life and death of Jesus foolishness, the converted subject finds in the cross and resurrection both the strength to reject that wisdom and the firm hope that his or her self-sacrifice will not prove futile. The authenticity of our response to Jesus' injunction to love God above all else finds its verification in the decisions and actions by which we follow Jesus in costly self-transcending love for the neighbor both within and outside the Christian community. Christian conversion unfolds as our self-transcending love adheres to the demands of God's love in Jesus (Mark), in the Church (Matthew), and in the world (Luke-Acts). The process of Christian conversion and development is distorted or stifled by the failure to respond to the demand of God's gift of love for continuing theocentric self-transcendence in Christ and his Church for all humankind.

The four Gospels serve as the norm for following Jesus within his community. They indicate the four consecutive phases that are essential to the fulfillment of the Christian conversion and maturation process. The lived achievement of one phase is called forth to the achievement of the next. Failure to respond to the summons for further theocentric self-transcendence in Christ and his Spirit jeopardizes present achievements. The basic temptation to self-sufficiency, to making oneself the ultimate guarantor of one's well-being and security, threatens to short-circuit the authentic development of the conversion and maturation process. Membership within the Christian community, in terms of a gratifying role within that community, may be used as a solution to the problems of life.

Another form of self-seeking is a legalism in which the concern with rectitude is the expression of the urge to self-justification rather than of theocentric self-transcendence. There is a search for "religious experience" that tends to make God the instrument for the fulfillment of one's wishes. With the Gnostic deviation, religious knowledge is understood and sought as a personal possession that enables one to be master of one's own destiny, to take control of one's eschatological fulfillment. Because Christianity is not a mere worldliness, but a holy worldliness, it is distorted if it is reduced to a mere social gospel. Fanatic apocalyptic mysticisms, formalism, illuminism, quietism, and sectarianism are among the many aberrations that frustrate the Christian conversion and maturation process, when the love of God is not strictly associated with an authentically Christocentric self-transcendence.

The Christian community preached the good news of God's love for us in its crucified and risen Lord. The acceptance of this good news, or gospel, entailed a conversion *(metanoia)*, thematized under the rubric of becoming a follower of Jesus. Christian preaching proclaimed such conversion and discipleship as normative for both the authentic fulfillment of human life and for deliverance from our incapacity to break away from our own evil ways. The call to follow Jesus is an invitation to accept the grace and demand of God's love for us the way that Jesus accepted it as the integrating center of his life. The New Testament thematizes the meaning of Christian conversion, the demand of the unrestricted love that the Christian has received and accepted as the integrating center of his or her life.

The New Testament teaches us to identify the ultimate source and term of that love as the Father of Jesus Christ; it points to Jesus as the revelation of the Father who completes his mission by sending the Spirit of their love for us. The New Testament symbolizes the realm of interpersonal divine life in terms of Jesus' relationship to his Father and Spirit. Authentic human fulfillment and redemption through the gift of God's love for us in Jesus Christ and his Spirit is interpreted in interpersonal terms. In this context, sin is understood as some form of impersonalism: the failure to be attentive, grateful, responsible, compassionate, merciful, faithful, reliable, and so on. Letting God be God consists in accepting the sovereignty of his love and the coming of the kingdom governed by that love. God alone actually loves *all* persons. Our finite, limited, human love is inadequate to the challenge of loving all persons, apart from the gift of God's all-embracing, all-encompassing, all-sustaining, all-reconciling, and all-fulfilling love. His community-creating love for all is the origin and ground of life in the kingdom that is entered by following Jesus' way of the cross in self-transcending theocentric love for all others. As the body of Christ and the temple of the Spirit, the Church is the sacrament of the Father's love for the integration of all humankind within the triune communion. The Church proclaims the way of the cross as the good news of the self-giving triune God integrating and transforming all humankind in his eternal life and love. This world can neither give nor take that life and love from us.

The passion and death of Jesus constitute the major event of each Gospel narrative because the cross reveals the truth of God's boundless love for us and verifies our love for one another. It is the measure of our commitment in freedom and love to all others. The crucified and risen Jesus is with his Spirit given to us the Father's loving self-investment in every human life for the coming of his kingdom. The compassion and passion of Jesus reveal God's making a gift of possibilities for a new life in the fullness of his own. The way of the cross is the way of that divine and human love that is eternal life in the kingdom of God.

The vision of world peace and universal love is an illusion apart from the triune God's self-gift that alone enables us to be reconciled and live in peace with ourselves and others with the triune communion. As long as we are our own little gods, refusing to let God be our God, we are not only alienated from but at odds with one another, each behaving like King Baby, as egocentric infants, each the center of the world, crying out for immediate satisfaction and imperiously demanding total attention from other King Babies who are equally frustrating and frustrated. The human ego as King Baby must die to itself to find its real self in communion with others; and this is impossible without our welcoming the Holy Spirit of divine life in the triune communion that frees us from our primordial infantilism for the fullness of life with all others. An ancient Near Eastern myth captures the ridiculous and absurd dimension of human egoism in telling of a person who attempts to sit comfortably on the royal throne, frantically trying to make his feet reach the floor and his hands reach the arms of the throne. The myth affirms that the King Baby in all of us is equally ridiculous, absurd, neurotically upset, and frantic because it is trying to fill a throne that it cannot occupy apart from communion with God and all others under the sovereignty of God's love. We are called to our place or "throne" in the kingdom of God; this is our peace and our dignity. Our real self is in communion with God and with all others. We face a fundamental choice in all our relatedness: alienation (sin) or loving union. In the Christian tradition, the person moves toward perfection by transforming all relations into relations of love, rooted and grounded in the love we welcome from our Father in Jesus Christ and the outpouring of their Spirit.

Personal growth and integration of all the facets of one's self are a possibility but not an inevitability. As a possibility, it is not simply a self-initiated project of self-perfection, but a gift of the Spirit by which personal development is transformed and integrated into the very life of the Trinity (triune communion).

CHAPTER EIGHT

Questions for Communion

The two questions that Paul asks when he finds himself confronted by God on the road to Damascus are at the heart of every Christian conversion experience both as event and as lifelong process:

1. "Who are you, Lord?" (Acts 22:8).
2. "What shall I do, Lord?" (Acts 22:10).

First, he must know who this God is who confronts him; then he must do something about it. Since God is that kind of God, Paul seems to be saying, *therefore* I must find out and do whatever he commands me to do. To "know" the living God, in the biblical sense, is to live with him in doing his will. Our action must be in response to God's action. We must be with God in doing what he is willing and doing. God loves us; *therefore* we must love one another (1 John 4:19). It would be absurd to talk about knowing God if you did not also love your brother.

Anyone who says "I love God" and hates his brother, is a liar, since a man who does not love the brother that he can see cannot love God, whom he has never seen. So this is the commandment that he has given us, that anyone who loves God must also love his brother (1 John 4:20-21).

Our desire to know God is authenticated by our seeking to know and to do his will within the complexity and historical particularities of our intrapersonal, interpersonal, social, national, and international life. We cannot know God apart from all the levels of human life; for through his grace and demands he is operative at every level.

Throughout the New Testament we find that a long passage about God will typically conclude with a "therefore," which goes on to point out how the knowledge of God is one with seeking to do his will. Sharing his life means doing his will.

In his letter to the Romans, for example, Paul writes eleven "theological" chapters, explaining who Jesus Christ is and what he has done for us. Then chapter 12 begins, "I appeal to you, *therefore*, my brothers," and Paul gives a long list of attitudes, practices, and characteristics of the way in which Christians are to act: Let love be genuine. Hate what is evil. Hold fast to what is good. Love one another with brotherly affection. Bless those who persecute you. Live in harmony with one another. Repay no one evil for evil. And the word "therefore" is the pivot of the whole argument. Because if all these things that I [Paul] have been writing to you about (for eleven chapters!) are true, Paul is saying in effect: *therefore*, this is the way in which you must act fully to experience true goodness for yourselves.

The Letter to the Ephesians offers another example. The first three chapters expound the work of Christ upon the cross, and the fourth begins:

"I, *therefore*, a prisoner in the Lord, implore you to lead a life worthy of your vocation. Bear with one another charitably, in complete selflessness, gentleness and patience. Do all you can to preserve the unity of the Spirit by the peace that binds you together" (4:1-3).

And the writer continues with advice about the way life is to be lived *because* of what God had done in Christ. We will know Christ and his Father only when we follow Christ in doing the will of his Father. Another striking example of this truth is found in Paul's Letter to the Philippians:

"Do nothing from selfishness or conceit, but in humility count others better than yourselves. Let each of you look not only to his own interests, but also to the interests of others. Have this mind among yourselves, which you have in Christ Jesus, who, though he was in the form of God, did not count equality with God a thing to be grasped, but emptied himself, taking the form of a servant, being born in the likeness of men. And being found in human form he humbled himself and became obedient unto death, even death on a cross" (2:3-8).

An assertion of what Christ has done is also an assertion of what we must do to know, in the biblical sense, who God is. God has acted in this way toward us; *therefore,* we are to act this way towards others. God loves us, and we shall give that same love to others if we truly "know" God. One who knows God will not refuse to love one whom God loves. What God wills is what he loves. God is known, in the biblical sense, in doing what he wills or loves. In Jesus Christ we have the ongoing answer of an infinitely knowing and loving God to *our* ongoing questions "Who are you?" and "What must I do?" The Christian desire to know the God of Jesus Christ is a daily quest inspired by the gift of his Spirit to know and to do his will. The Spirit of Jesus Christ and his Father unites and animates the Christian community in its thirst for God and for the accomplishment of his will. It expresses itself in the community's prayer. "Thy kingdom come, thy will be done." The community prays that it may increasingly come to know God in faith, and acknowledge him as the holy center and meaning of its life. Its prayer expresses its belief that God's purpose is to unite all human hearts under the sovereignty of his love. The life and teaching of Jesus spell out what the Christian community believes the doing of God's will and the coming of his kingdom entails.

The Christian community believes that God's will for us is always his love for us. God wills always and only what is best for us and for all others. We cannot will anything better for ourselves than God's will for us because he loves us infinitely more than we can love ourselves. To think that we love ourselves more than God does is a failure to believe and to trust in his infinite love for us. Our unfaith leads us to think that we know better than God what is good for ourselves because we cannot believe that he really knows and loves us infinitely more than we know and love ourselves. God loves us truly because he knows us as we truly are. Because our self-knowledge is always limited, we can never love ourselves as truly as God does.

The Question-raising God

The biblical narratives are an external expression of the interior life of a covenant people. The questions that God raises in these narratives reveal what is going on in the cognitive and affective life of people at every level: intrapersonal, interpersonal, social, national and international. There is no knowing God, in the biblical sense, without experiencing him as a question-raising God at every level of human life. He reveals himself in the questions he raises about our lives. His question-raising reality is experienced wherever and whenever we seriously ask about the ultimate meaning and goodness of our lives. God is as inescapable as his questions. Significantly, God's first word to us in the Bible is a question: "Where are you?" (Gen 3:9). The covenant people experiences God in his question about its identity. Its quest for God begins with its experience of his quest or question for them. To hear his word is to hear his question about the meaning and purpose and goodness of its life. The people of the New Covenant hears that question-raising word in Jesus Christ, whose first utterance in the Gospels of Luke and John is a question: "Why were you looking for me?" (Luke 2:49), and "What do you want?" (John 1:38).

From the moment of the annunciation, God's word is a question-raising event in Luke's Gospel: "She was deeply troubled by these words and asked herself what this greeting could mean" (1:30); and "How can this come about, since I am a virgin?" (1:34). Mary experiences the question-raising mystery of her son when she finds him in the temple and asks, "My child, why have you done this to us?" (2:48).

The entire life story of God's incarnate Word challenges us as God's question and answer about our identity. Jesus Christ is the incarnate Question and Answer of God about the true goodness and direction of our lives. Even the shortest Gospel, Mark, reflects the tension of the Question that Jesus is for all human life with its no less than one hundred eighteen questions, of which more than half are raised by Jesus himself.

If the Gospel narrative is the external expression of knowing and loving Christian subject (the evangelist) in the lifelong process of conversion, the questions that pervade it imply that an authentically Christian life is one of loving responsiveness to the question-raising meaning of God at every level of human life. If the Church employs this narrative in its pedagogy for cultivating the gift of God's love in the interests of human transformation (conversion) at every level, it implicitly recognizes the dynamic of the question for learning to know God in the biblical sense as the question-raising Mystery at the heart of all human life. Christian maturation, then, implies fidelity to the question that God raises and to the answer that he gives about the true meaning and goodness of our lives. If God is known by doing his will, the Christian must learn to live in the daily tension of the question "What is God's will for me?"; There is no doing God's will without seeking it in the concreteness and complexity of our lives. (The self-righteous are their own "little gods"; they evade his question by implicitly identifying God's will with their own self-will.)

Being with Jesus, or Christian discipleship, entails following him in learning to live with responding love to the question-raising Mystery (God) at the heart of all human life. It means accepting the Question that is God himself, of seeking to know and to do his will. We accept our true and God-given identity in doing his will. The kingdom of God—life under the sovereignty of his love—is coming wherever his will is being done. If God's will is done, all human persons will enjoy the fulfillment of their true interpersonal identity in his kingdom. We are free to reject our God-given identity in favor of self-will, where the self is king in its own impersonal kingdom. There is no authentically interpersonal life where the sovereignty of God's love is rejected. Jesus' "thy will, not mine" (Luke 22:42) expresses the radical responsibility to God that grounds freedom for genuinely interpersonal life. His way of the cross reveals his acceptance of his God-given identity as the "Beloved Son"; this is his way of self-transcendence as the Beloved Son that he is glad to be in responding (responsible) love with his Father. His way of the cross reveals how his disciples must accept their God-given identity.

The dynamic of the question in the Gospel narrative is ultimately that of God's love flooding our hearts through the Holy Spirit given to us (Rom 5:5), for the narrative is a symbolic expression and witness to the Christian community's knowledge (in the biblical sense) of that love manifested in Jesus Christ and communicated through his Spirit. The Gospel narrative is implicitly the Christian community's answer to the question "What does it mean to love God with one's whole heart and whole soul, with all one's mind and all one's strength?" (Mark 12:30). What does it mean to fulfill the new commandment of Jesus, "Love one another just as I have loved you" (John 15:12)? What is God's distinctive way of loving as manifested in Jesus Christ and in the believing community that lives in his Spirit? How ought we to respond to that love? What is God doing in my life?

The Gospel writers employ the dynamic of the question to symbolize the pattern of God's love and its distinctive way of operating in our lives. Love is the central motivation of the question-raising and question-answering dynamic of the Gospel narrative. The Gospel writers implicitly reply to the question. "What is the appropriate response to our being loved by God in Christ and his Spirit?" They present Jesus as the norm that we are to follow for such a response. His "Come, follow me" (Mark 1:16) expresses the dynamic of divine initiative and human response at the heart of our transformation in the lifelong process of our learning to live in God's love. Following Jesus in response to the grace and demand of God's love constitutes Christian conversion both as event and lifelong process.

Such conversion is always precarious; for we can fall out of love with God. Consequently, we are bid to watch and pray, to make our way in fear and trembling. We can always fail to heed Jesus' invitation to follow him in his self-surrender to his Father's love. His invitation raises the question daily, "Are we following Jesus in response to God's love?" The Gospel narrative was written to raise the question for all Christians at all times: "Are we living in the Spirit of Jesus, leading lives of responding love?" Hearing God's Word means hearing his question and responding appropriately. Raising the question implies that no Christian should self-righteously assume that he or she is always following Jesus; for God alone is unquestionably good. Although our lives are the manifestation of God's grace, they are measured by the demands of his intention.

The Church employs the dynamic of the question in the Gospel narrative for its spiritual pedagogy. We must learn to hear the Question and the Answer (God) that is at the heart of every human life in order to become authentically human, following Jesus' way of responding love to human and divine others. That question must always challenge our self-understanding, individually and socially, and be the norm of our decision and action. The Word of God takes the form of the Question and the Answer that is given to us in Jesus Christ and his Spirit. That Word expresses the Spirit of the Father's love that has been given to us and elicits our responding through and in the same Spirit of love to the Question and the Answer that constitutes our God-given identity. Our hearing the Question (in the biblical sense of a loving response to the grace and demand of God) is even now our accepting the Answer that is our God-given interpersonal identity. The just are even now rising in responding love to the Question that is also the Answer to their identity. The dynamic of the Question in the Gospel narrative implies the Christian community's grateful response to that enduring love that it knows in its fidelity to the Spirit.

Every New Testament affirmation about God is implicitly the Christian community's answer of responding love to the Word that is both the question and answer of God. Jewish and Christian Scriptures are the expression of responding love inspired by the gift of the Spirit of love for the God who speaks in his question and answer. Paul affirms that Jesus Christ is the *Yes* spoken by God in response to the implicit question of Israel: Is God faithful? (2 Cor 1:20). This corresponds to John's doctrine of Christ as the *Amen* (Rev 3:14).

John's doctrine of the Son as the Word of God who is the fullness of truth (prologue to his Gospel) implies his life of responding love for the question that is the self-revealing answer. John's living in the Spirit of love for the question of God yields the answer of God. He knows the Spirit (in the biblical sense) in the love that the members of the New Covenant community have for one another. On the basis of their loving correspondence for one another before the Word-Question-Answer of God, John can affirm that "God is love" (1 John 4:8, 16).

The Father communicates himself by sending his Son (Word) and Spirit (Love). He speaks his Word of truth and Spirit of love, empowering us in the special biblical sense to know him and to accept our true identity. There is no hearing or lived experience of the Father's Word, as question or answer, apart from the Spirit of his love through and in which his will becomes our meaningful life-principle. Jesus is known as Lord (1 Cor 12:3) in the biblical sense only by those whose hearts and minds are governed by the Holy Spirit of his love; his meaning as God's Word is effectively grasped only by those who live in the Spirit of his love for the Father. The Gospel narrative of the way of the cross implicitly answers the question of Jesus' meaning for us. It symbolizes what it means to have an authentically interpersonal life with God and all others. There is no such life without the self-transcendence of responding love for all others, divine and human.

The dynamic of the question in the Gospel narrative is indispensable for Christian conversion both as event and as a lifelong process of maturation; for there is no human transformation or maturation, at any level, without questions. Because we are neither self-explanatory nor self-sufficient, we must go outside ourselves in self-transcendence for both our meaning and our fulfillment. The quest for both takes the form of the question. The dynamic of our questioning implies that we are not autonomous, but relational beings, seeking the answers correlative to our questions. The same dynamic implies a correspondence of knowing and loving subjects. If we are able and willing to question, there must be others who are able and willing to answer. Our questioning presupposes answerable and responsible (response-able) others. Reciprocity is possible among knowing subjects who are able to question and to answer, and loving subjects who are willing to question and to answer. If persons are knowing and loving subjects, their authenticity is achieved in co-responsibility. Persons are interpersonal or conscious and relational; consequently the failure to be interpersonal is the failure to be personal. Irresponsibility is the failure to be a knowing and loving subject.

Our personal identity is interpersonal, and it is rooted in co-responsibility. It is defined by those to and for whom we are responsible (answerable). The Good News of Jesus Christ is the perfection of divine and human co-responsibility. He is the response (answer) of the knowing and loving Father to our human need for him; and he is the response of perfect human receptivity to and availability for the Father. He is the Good News that God assumes responsibility for, for the fulfillment of every human life; that God sends his Son and his Spirit for that purpose. He is the Good News of God's responding love to the need of every human person for him, and of man's perfectly corresponding availability for God's love. The interpersonal life of Jesus Christ is the solidarity of God and humankind in corresponding (co-responsible) love. He is both the prayer of all humankind for God and the response of God to that prayer. Significantly, all the evangelists show Jesus, before all the great decisions of his life, spending the night in prayer alone on the mountain.

There is no passivity in Jesus' receptivity, response, and listening to his Father. His receptivity is at one and the same time supreme activity, commitment to accept demands, making himself available, and being ready to serve in responding love. Solidity or co-responsibility with God demands the supreme activity of his self-giving in commitment to his Father's will. At Gethsemane he prays: "Abba, Father, all things are possible for you. Take this cup away from me. But let it be as you, not I, would have it" (Mark 14:36).

Always doing what is pleasing to his Father (John 8:29), Jesus is a knowing and loving subject who co-responsibly collaborates with his Father in giving the new life of their Holy Spirit to all others. Christian discipleship consists in our being with Jesus in his costly and supreme activity of receiving his life from the Father and communicating it to others as fully co-responsible knowing and loving subjects living in his Spirit. Through the gift of his Spirit we are invited and empowered to share the freedom of Jesus Christ's co-responsibility with the Father and all others. Actively accepting the Holy Spirit as our new life-principle, we accept our God-given identity as co-responsible knowing and loving subjects and the freedom for an authentically interpersonal fulfillment. Through the gift of the Holy Spirit we are free to share in the interpersonal co-responsibility and life-principle of the knowing and loving subject that is Jesus Christ.

The Gospel writers employ the dynamic of the question to evoke the co-responsibility of their readers. They have written their question-raising narratives as a call to co-responsibility with God in Christ and his Spirit for others. The co-responsibility of New Covenant brothers and sisters for one another and all others reveals the co-responsibility of the covenant-creating and covenant-sustaining Spirit of Jesus Christ and his Father. The Spirit of love with which the Son responds to the Father and with which the Father responds to the Son is made manifest among those who respond to one another with the same love. The Father and the Son are wherever their Spirit is operative in the co-responsible activity of all who receive it to become covenant-creating and covenant-sustaining persons. Such persons respond to the Word, whether as Question or Answer, that God speaks within their life story, by becoming the communicators of faith and hope for others. They communicate complementary aspects of the grace and demand of that Word for authentic human development and fulfillment under the sovereignty of God's corresponding love in response to human need.

The costly commitment of Christians to God in the service of others both within the realm of covenant community responsibilities and the world beyond is rooted in the mutual indwelling and self-transcending love of the Father and Son that constitutes the community of Christian faith. The out-going compassion of Christians for others without limits or conditions bears witness to the indwelling Trinitarian love that is the ultimate source and term of the Christian community's life and that of the world that it is called to serve in co-responsibility with the three Persons. The giving of new life is the very meaning of the dynamic of the question at the heart of all human life. The meaning of the Gospel is revealed in this dynamic within the realms of our experience, understanding, judgment, decision, and action, where the Word of God summons us to co-responsibility. Jesus' first words in Luke (2:49) and John (1:38) are, respectively, the questions: "Why were you looking for me?" and "What do you want?"

Just as in the measure that we advert to our own questioning and proceed to question it, there arises the question of God.[1] So, too, in the measure that we advert to our being questioned by God and proceed to respond, there arises the question of our authenticity. We achieve authenticity in the self-transcendence whereby we become knowing and loving subjects whose cognition and affectivity are concomitantly experienced in our unrestricted drive to know and to love. In the Gospel narratives, Jesus questions us to stimulate our questioning, reflection, response, and conversion to unrestricted loving. Jesus summons us to the unrestricted questioning and loving that would free us from being locked up in ourselves. As the question of God is implicit in all our questioning, so being in love with God is the basic fulfillment of our conscious intentionality as knowing and loving subjects.[2]

The biblical narrative presents questions for intelligence or understanding, reflecting the life of the People of God asking what and why and how and what for: "When the Israelites saw it [food in the desert], they said to one another, 'What is it?'—for they did not know what it was" (Exod 16:15).[3] In the wonder created by Jesus' first miracle, Mark records that "They were dumbfounded and began to ask one another, 'What is this?' " (1:27). The occurrence of Mary's questions is striking in Luke: "Why have you treated us like this?" (2:48), and "How can this be . . . when I have no husband?" (1:34). Nathanael asks: "How do you come to know me?" (John 1:48). Jesus asks: "If I spoke well, why strike me?" (John 18:23). A more reflective attitude indicating the inner tension of inquiry, the dynamisms of the search for understanding, occurs when Luke tells us that: "Mary treasured all these things and pondered over them" (2:19). The word "pondered" is the same one he uses for the "discussion" of the Jewish rulers on how to handle Peter and John (Acts 4:15), and for the "debate" in which the Athenian philosophers engaged Paul (Acts 17:18). Linked with this is the occurrence of wonder in its milder forms, as when outside the sanctuary "the people were waiting for Zechariah, wondering why he was staying so long inside" (Luke 1:21).

Upon questions for intelligence and understanding follow questions for reflection, asking whether or not this really is so or that really could be. This question regards truth, what is so. It requires evidence enough to justify a judgment on the matter; it asks which side of a contradiction is right. John presents some instances: "There was much whispering about him in the crowds. 'He is a good man,'

some said. 'No,' said others, 'He is leading the people astray' "
(7:12). Later we have the significant statement: "Thus he caused
a split among the people" (7:43). John's affirmation that "Jesus is
the Christ, the Son of God" (20:31) raises a question for reflection
that leads to the split of Christ's followers from Judaism. The high
priest challenges Jesus with such a question: "By the living God
I charge you to tell us: Are you the Messiah, the Son of God?" (Matt
26:63). The same question for reflection is implied in the centurion's
affirmation: "Truly this man was the Son of God" (Mark 15:39).
Jesus' cross-questioning of the Pharisees provides another instance
of the same type of question: "Whose son is he (the Messiah)? 'The
son of David,' they replied . . . 'If David calls him "Lord," how
can he be David's son?' " (Matt 22:42-45).

Questions arise in the order of doing as well as knowing. Questions for deliberation arise when we ask whether this or that is
worthwhile, whether it is not just apparently good but truly good,
what has objective value. Jesus' statements "Go and do the same
yourself" (Luke 10:37), and "Mary has chosen the better part"
(10:42), and ". . . do this and life is yours" (Luke 10:28) answer
questions for deliberation.

Jesus poses questions for identity: "Who is my mother? Who are
my brothers?" (Mark 3:33); "What is your name?" (Mark 5:9); "Who
do you say I am?" (Mark 8:29). He poses questions for intelligence
or understanding: "Why are you frightened? Have you still no
faith?" (Mark 4:40); "Where did he get all this? What wisdom is
this that has been given him? How does he perform miracles? Isn't
he the carpenter, the son of Mary . . .?" (Mark 6:2-3). He raises
the question about what people are doing and where they are going, about the meaning of their life: "You have eyes, can't you see?
You have ears, can't you hear?" (Mark 8:18) and "Can you see anything?" (Mark 8:23). Questions define the relationship between the
Master and the disciple; for the true understanding of discipleship
is co-relative to the true understanding of the Master. When Peter
acknowledges that Jesus is the Christ and then immediately rejects
Jesus' way of suffering and death, he reveals his failure to understand the true meaning of both the Master and of discipleship (Mark
8:27-9:1).[4] At a deeper level, the failure to grasp Jesus' true mean-

ing is the failure to grasp our own God-given identity. Jesus is the answer of God to the question of what we are called to be.

Our sincere engagement with the question is already a form of commitment to the answer. The questions that are most important to us concern the matters that are dearest to us. There are no such questions apart from the effective power and motivation that sustains them. Love seeks understanding. Love asks all she meets, as we read in the Song of Solomon, where she can find her Lover. A loving heart is a questioning heart; an indifferent heart knows no such interest. Even the questions of Jesus' adversaries show that they are not indifferent and are therefore at least in touch with the love that could save them.

Our lives are qualified by the quality of the questions that engage us. Preoccupation with trivial questions and concerns trivializes our lives. The Christian community employs its Gospel narrative to learn to live with the most fundamental questions about human life and to respond to them in the Spirit of Jesus Christ. The answers to the basic questions that Jesus Christ raises are given to those who are willing to share his life of costly self-transcendence or way of the cross. The answers to his questions are learned in the authentic co-responsibility of those who live in the Spirit of Jesus Christ within his New Covenant community.

The New Covenant community gives witness to its Lord by becoming the question-raising and answer-giving sacrament of God for the world. The Word of God, both as question and answer, is spoken to the world in and through the New Covenant community. The three Persons reveal and communicate their co-responsibility in the life of the New Covenant community for all humankind.

Covenant love is co-responsible love both among covenant members and between them and all others, human and divine. The covenant love of Jesus Christ is known, in the biblical sense, by those who accept with responding love his brothers and sisters, no less than his Father and Spirit. His interpersonal life of covenant love reveals an interpersonal God as a community of Persons living in responding love and co-responsibly creating and sustaining and fulfilling all humankind through the grace and summons to co-responsibility. Their co-responsible love is the gift and summons for ours.

The dynamic of the question in the Gospel narrative represents a co-responsible Father and Son and Spirit (uncreated grace of self-gift) summoning us to the co-responsibility of an authentically human life, to "knowing God" (in the biblical sense) in loving all others. The dynamic of the question is an implicit summons to the way of the cross; for without the costly responding love that is self-transcendence, we cannot become co-responsible and "know God."

Rejection of the cross is radical irresponsibility in the refusal to become seriously engaged with the answer that Jesus offers in the question that he raises about the ultimate meaning and value of human life; for there is no human authenticity apart from self-transcendence in communion with the Spirit of the Father and Son that enables it. The Word that is question draws us to itself as answer in the tension of co-responsible love that the Gospel narrative represents as Jesus Christ's way of the cross. The Spirit of that Word has been given to enable our hearing that Word both as question (promise) and answer (fulfillment), as the Alpha and the Omega of every human story. The Spirit is wherever it acts, and it acts in the lives of co-responsible persons responding wholeheartedly to Jesus' commandment of love (Matt 22:34-40; Mark 12:28-34; Luke 10:25-28). The love of God finds expression in the love of neighbor, and the love of neighbor receives its foundation and energy in the love of God that is given to us in the Spirit of the Father and his Son. Wherever that Spirit is being accepted, co-responsible persons are accepting in responding love the answer to the question that is the origin and ground and direction and the fulfillment of all human life.

Irresponsibility can be regarded as our futile attempt to give ourselves a meaning that implies our radical rejection of our God-given meaning. We can futilely attempt to take our life stories "out of context" with respect to the question and answer that is their ultimate background, ground, and foreground. We can attempt to make our own human egos the ultimate context of our human story.

To take anything out of context is to lose its true meaning. The rationalizations of a bad conscience express the experience of such a taking-out-of-context. The discomfort and unease of a bad conscience is the voice of God recalling us to the true meaning of our life story. Our radical misinterpretation of the universal human story and its ultimate context (God) distorts our grasp of all human stories by taking them out of their true context, that which ultimately makes them truly good and meaningful. God alone is the answer to our quest for our true meaning and goodness. Because God addresses himself to every human being, we are enabled to be free, conscious, co-responsible, knowing and loving subjects (persons) whose existence as such is constituted by the endless answer to the question that grounds our lives.

Jesus asks 98 different questions in the synoptic Gospels. He raises twelve additional questions in his parables. Forty-seven different questions are addressed to Jesus in these Gospels. Of the approximately 157 questions raised in the synoptic Gospels, 110 originate with Jesus himself. Even the 47 questions addressed to Jesus are occasioned by him. The healing context of many questions suggests their importance in the psychotherapeutic dialogue of faith and trust. The dynamic of the question lies at the heart of human transformation in the event and lifelong process of Christian conversion. Jesus' questions challenge us to growth and development at every level (intrapersonal, interpersonal and social) under God.

A Gnostic pattern is present in the Gospel of Thomas, where the emphasis is on Jesus as the one who answers all our questions about mysteries, whereas in the New Testament, the emphasis is on Jesus as the one who raises questions for our responsible decision and action, calling us to new life, to sell all, and to follow him in the self-transcendence of total surrender to God.

Our Questions and Our Desire to Know God

Every act of questioning presupposes the possibility of our finding the truth. Without an implicit "faith" that intelligibility and truth can be found, we would not have the courage to seek understanding or to make judgments about the world around us. By the fact that we do ask questions and make judgments (even, for example, "it is a truth that there is no intelligibility or truth") we give ample evidence that we cannot eradicate our primordial trust in the intelligibility and truth of reality. That we find ourselves spontaneously asking questions is direct evidence for the fact of our having a desire to know the truth.

But there are different types of questions. Some of our questions inquire as to what a thing is or ask about its meaning, intelligibility or significance. This type of question is resolved when we are given an "insight" into the essence of something. If you find yourself asking what the author of this book is trying to convey in these sentences, then this is an example of the first type of question. It may be called a "question for understanding." It will reach its goal when you find yourself saying: "Now I see the point."

But gaining understanding is not the end of the questioning process. For not every insight is in touch with reality. There can be illusory as well as realistic understanding. So a second type of question spontaneously arises, and it leads you to ask whether your insights or those of others are true. I may see the point that an author is trying to make, but an uneasiness will eventually lead me to ask whether this point is well-taken. Is it faithful to the facts of my own experience? Is it based on reality? Is it true? This type of questioning provides evidence that I am not content with mere insight and understanding. Thus I ask: Is it really so? Does this viewpoint correspond with reality? Is it a fact? We may call this second type "question for reflection" or a "critical question." It is especially our critical questions that give evidence of our desire to know and of our basic discontent with mere understanding. We want to make sure that our insights, hypotheses, and theories are true to reality.

Asking a question is possible because we do not yet know the answer. If we knew the answer we would not ask the question in the first place. And yet we know something about what we are questioning in order to ask about it at all. But at the same time our consciousness has to dwell within the horizon of truth in order for us to inquire about it at all. In other words, our minds must already have moved into a specific field of knowledge and been influenced by the objects of this field in order for us to ask about what lies within the horizon. I could not seriously desire the truth about myself, others, and the world unless the horizon of truth had already encircled my consciousness.

If we know that God means truth, our affirmation of this ultimate horizon cannot, by definition, be an illusion. For the desire for the truth undercuts all illusions. If we identify "God" with the unrestricted horizon of truth and love toward which our desire to know is directed, we need not fear that our belief is a projection of wishful thinking. If the desire for God is at root the desire for truth, then this desire will not be able to take refuge in illusions or mere thinking.

The desire for God coincides with our desire for truth. God is the ultimate horizon of truth that continually activates our desire to ask questions and allows us no peace until we have surrendered to it. God is the ultimate objective of all our questioning. Truth is ultimately a *mysterium tremendum et fascinans*.[5] As in the case of the "sacred," we both hide from it and seek it at the same time. We know that the truth hurts, but we also intuit that it alone can provide a firm foundation to our lives. The ultimate truth, depth, future, freedom, and beauty into whose embrace we are constantly invited consists of an unconditional love that is the *tremendum* from which we flee as well as the *fascinans* that promises us ultimate fulfillment. If we find the elusiveness or depth or "futurity" of truth intolerable, it may be because our strong impulse to master takes precedence over our desire to be grasped by the truth.

Religion may be understood as the conscious decision to move within the truth. It is a rejection of the strong temptation to make truth the object of our will to mastery. It is a surrender to truth as the *mysterium tremendum et fascinans* in which alone our freedom and fulfillment lie. Religion is an ongoing conversion to the dimension of the truth that transcends the everyday world of fear and all the illusions based on fear. Wherever there is a sincere desire for the truth about ourselves, others, and the world, there is authentic religion, even if it does not go by that name. The religiousness of their desire for the truth consists of a fundamental trust in the ultimate intelligibility of reality without which we would not have the courage to ask questions and to seek the truth. From the perspective of human consciousness and longing, religion has its origins essentially in the God-given desire for the truth, i.e., God himself. The core of religion is an uncompromising passion for the truth.

If mystery is understood merely as a vacuum that begs to be filled with our intellectual achievements and not as an ineffable depth summoning us to surrender ourselves completely to it, then it is hardly adequate as a term for the divine. The gaps in our present understanding and knowledge would better be called "problems" than mysteries. A "problem" can eventually be solved by the application of human ingenuity. Mystery, in contrast to problems, is incapable of any "solution." Mystery becomes more prominent the deeper our questions go and the surer our answers become. Mystery appears to consciousness at the "limit" of our ordinary problem-oriented questions. It reveals itself decisively at the point where we seriously ask what may be called "limited-questions," questions that lie at the "boundary" of our ordinary problem-solving consciousness.

For example, while science is dominated by problems for which some resolution or definitive answer is expected, the scientist might find himself eventually asking: Why should I do science at all? Why search for intelligibility in the universe? Similarly, the field of ethics attempts to give answers to our moral dilemmas; but at the limits of ethical investigation there arise such questions as: Why bother about ethics at all? Why be responsible? Why pursue the good life? Why keep promises? Why should we be faithful? Is the universe at heart faithful and trustworthy? If it is not, then why should I worry about fidelity and promise-keeping? At this juncture we have shifted from ethical problems into the realm of the mysterious and unsolvable. Ethics can no more easily answer these limiting questions than science can tell us why we should seek intelligibility in the universe.

Another illustration: literary criticism attempts to respond to questions concerning whether a work of literature is aesthetically worthy of our respect. But at the limit of literary criticism there arise questions that it cannot itself address: Why pursue the beautiful? Why bother about aesthetic criteria at all? What is beauty? Again we have moved out of problem and into mystery.

Each discipline is specified by the types of questions it raises, the kinds of problems with which it deals. It pursues its questions with a degree of success proportionate to the problems it solves. But at the boundaries of all these various fields of human inquiry we come to an impasse that we cannot get beyond no matter how much intellectual effort we exert. Our problem-solving techniques cannot get us over the encompassing horizon of mystery opened up by our limit-questions.

The place of mystery, and hence the appropriate place for the introduction of a specifically religious discourse, is at the limits of our problem-oriented questioning, when our inquiry shifts to another key entirely. At such a point we realize we are asking questions that no human ingenuity will ever solve or "remove." But even though we cannot give final solutions to these impossible questions, we may still respond (that is, "answer back") to them. This response is appropriately not one of trying to ignore, repress, or eliminate them, but rather allowing them to take over our consciousness and pull us into the mystery that lurks on the other side of our problems.

Besides the mysterious questions that arise at the limits of our intellectual life there are also the "boundary experiences" that confront us at the edges of our everyday life. The encounter with suffering, frustration, and ultimately death arouses questions of an entirely different sort from those we "normally" ask. Usually we are preoccupied with the ordinary "problems" of life, such as how to pay bills, how to pass a course, and so forth. In other words "how" questions dominate the ordinary course of our lives. But there are certain "shipwreck" or "earthquake" experiences that occasionally break into the routine of our lives, and when they do, we experience the superficiality of our pragmatic "how" questions and the invasion of "why" or "ultimate" questions. Such experiences raise questions that stand at the "limit" of our ordinary consciousness of life, and they can sensitize us to the mystery that always silently accompanies and encompasses our lives. When we are beset by these marginal experiences we ask "ultimate" questions more intently perhaps than before. Can this be all there is to life? Are death and tragedy the final word? Is there any final meaning to my work? Is there an answer to the problem of suffering? Perhaps the questions aroused by tragedy make us most vulnerable to the touch of mystery. Nevertheless, positive and ecstatic moments of deep joy can just as readily transport us beyond the boundaries of pedestrian existence.

The feeling of being deeply loved by another or of being enthralled by great beauty can also lead us to ask limit-questions. Will love prevail? Is beauty only an illusion? Why can't these moments last forever? Such questions open us to mystery and lead us to a religious interpretation of the universe. At the "limit" of our ordinary experience and our problem-solving questions we are alerted to the nearness of mystery. We sense that it has been intimately present all along but that it has not entered deeply into our explicit awareness. In limit-experience and limit-questioning we are confronted with the opportunity of making the dimension of mystery the most important and enlivening aspect of our lives.

CHAPTER NINE

Models for Communion

Human growth and development is a question of having the right heroes, models, saints, and leaders. From our earliest years we are shaped by our relationships to our parents and to the significant others whose life stories impinge upon our own. Our earliest conduct is imitative rather than deliberately learned and chosen. Before we can conceptualize our experience and evaluate it, before we can share the experiences of other times and places through reading, before we can share our own experiences with others through writing, we base our conduct upon the models who surround us. Anyone who has been present as a neutral observer in a family will testify how the parents' faults and behavior patterns are imitated and reproduced in their children, even though the parents may have verbally forbidden and disapproved of such modes of behavior. Before we become responsible for the models we choose as our own, our openness to truth and our commitment to value have been conditioned by the influence of those upon whom we most depend. We imitate those who surround us. We do not choose the initial models or patterns of human behavior with which we are presented.

We seldom, if ever, act according to principles and rules stated in words and logically arranged. Rather we act according to models and stories. Young children spontaneously ask their parents to tell the story of their own childhood so that it may shed light upon their own. Our behavior is imitative rather than rule-abiding; prior to our intention to obey sets of rules, we are trying to become a certain type of person.

William Kirk Kilpatrick, professor of educational psychology at Boston College, underscores the importance of stories of wisdom for teaching morality.[1] Long before the Greeks learned their ethics from Aristotle, they learned them from the *Iliad* and the *Odyssey*. When Christianity swept the world, it was the Gospel story, not the Christian ethic, that captured human hearts. Still later, people learned how to behave well by hearing accounts of the lives of saints and stories of Arthur, Percival, and Galahad. These stories are good teaching devices, and our own lives are best understood as stories. An individual is more than just an individual self. The individual belongs to an ongoing tradition, a family story or a tribal story. We cannot identify ourselves without bringing in the whole family history. We are defined by the story of which we are a part. We each play an irreplaceable part in a cosmic drama, a story in which some of the strands come together only in eternity. In such a story, what you do counts infinitely. A traditional incentive to moral behavior was the conviction that we are part of a story that begins before us and goes on after us, but whose outcome we may influence. The important thing was to play our part well in the ongoing enterprise to which all belonged.

Certain things are expected of those who want to play a part in the Christian Story. The main reason that you cannot extract ethical principles from Christianity and set them up on their own is that Christianity is *not* an ethical system. It is not meant to be a prescription for good behavior, although good behavior is one of its side effects. It is a true and good life story. Consequently, it makes no sense to talk about keeping the Christian ethic and ignoring Christ. The story is mainly about Christ: who he is and what he has done. Without him it makes no sense. You cannot separate the message of Christ from the person of Christ and simply pretend that his words are equally meaningful in any good person's mouth. "I am the Resurrection and the Life" and "Before Abraham came to be, I Am" are lines that belong to the life story of one Person. Our doing the right thing is no guarantee that others will do so. Our role is to play our part faithfully and as best we can see it in the light of Christian faith and hope and love. The traditional morality of character gives us good people as models and asks us to act like them; it provides us with life stories to live by.

In our quest for models, heroes, saints, and leaders, we desire candor, compassion, wisdom, and courage. There is a tendency to honor the hero in the figure of the conqueror and to forget the life story of Christ, in which genuine fortitude or courage means precisely to endure "wounds" on behalf of truth and justice (from loss of reputation or well-being to imprisonment or bodily harm.) Such a person does not vanquish, he sacrifices. Heroic fortitude, we learn in the Christ story, is more the virtue of the seemingly vanquished; it consists primarily in steadfast commitment and not in attacking. "Passion," as employed in the "Passion Story" of Christ, means suffering or enduring. Fortitude is a dimension of the strong and enduring love of patience. Martyrdom is the ultimate test of the invincible love that suffering, evil and death cannot overcome. The invincible love of the crucified Christ, the Son of God, expresses the distinctively Christian understanding of hero, saint, and leader. From the Christian standpoint, the steadfast love of the martyr has always been viewed as a victory of invincible love and commitment in confrontation with evil.

We cannot imagine heroes, models, saints, and leaders without the courage to make serious decisions. Often our reluctance to make serious decisions and commitments is less a fear of suffering than a secret dread of irreversible results that permit few illusions or certainties about what will follow. We share with Hamlet the tendency to postponement. We might, with Heyst in Joseph Conrad's *Victory*, choose drift: security by withdrawal and passivity. Ignoring the demands for responsible decisionmaking and commitment within our social situation can be a form of moral stagnation or death. A former president of General Motors, asked the reason of his remarkable success, replied that he had had the courage to make many decisions and that at least sixty percent of them were good ones.

In Aristotelian terms, a good leader must have *ethos*, *pathos*, and *logos*. The *ethos* is his moral character, the source of his ability to persuade: his moral authority. The *pathos* is his ability to touch feelings, to move people emotionally. The *logos* is his ability to give solid reasons for an action, to move people rationally or intellectually, so that their affectivity and action is well-ordered. Christians believe that God leads his people as the Father who sends his Son and Word *(Logos)* in a human nature and their Holy Spirit of love to transform human persons within the body of Christ and the temple of the Spirit (Church). The Church is the history of the triune God's communion with human persons; its inmost nature resides in the very nature of God. The inward communion of God the Father and Son and Spirit enables the outward communion of God and human persons. The authority of the Son derives from the Father, and he transforms human hearts through the gift of their Spirit. The Father "authorizes" his incarnate Son to lead all human persons into the eternal life and love of the triune communion through the gift of their Holy Spirit. Pius XII, in his Encyclical on the Mystical Body (1943), stressed the personal presence of the Holy Spirit in our souls, as in the soul of Christ our Leader. He dwells in our souls to perform gradually within us what he performed in Christ from the first moment: turning him entirely towards the Father in all that he said and did, both in his life as a priest, which led him to make a total sacrifice of himself to bring us, too, to the fullness of life within the Trinity.

The fortitude of heroes, saints, and leaders is a testimony to the existence of evil; for, in the world, evil is a powerful force. To be brave means that something must be risked whenever the obviously vulnerable offers resistance to evil. And no one who wishes to be a good human being, and who is unwilling to commit an injustice, can avoid this risk. Moral and spiritual excellence requires the effort of individuals and societies who are willing to struggle and if necessary to sacrifice on its behalf. It is a liberalistic illusion to believe that one can be consistently just, for example, without having to risk something for it. That is why fortitude is necessary. What is risked, if the occasion arises, may be something less than life itself. It may be instead a question of immediate well-being, of daily tranquillity, possessions, honor, or face-saving. On the other hand, what is required may be the surrender of life, or more exactly, the acceptance of death at another's hands.

The martyr is the ultimate symbol of fortitude and heroism. The moral steadfastness of the martyr has always been understood as a victory and celebrated as such, not only from the Christian standpoint but also from that of Plato's Socrates. "We conquer by being slain," wrote Tertullian. Who was ultimately the victor: the boasting commandant of Auschwitz or the Polish Franciscan father Maximilian Kolbe, who, in order to save a fellow man, went into the starvation bunker and perished there? In spite of all, the martyr is truly a hero, and so is every unimposing or unknown individual who risks his or her life for the sake of truth and good, whether in the dramatic act of martyrdom or in lifelong devotion and commitment—in acquiescence to the will of God at the cost of one's own worldly comfort. Teresa of Avila writes in her autobiography that an imperfect human being needs greater fortitude to travel the path of perfection than to take martyrdom upon him- or herself in a brief moment. Perhaps this affirmation, based upon life experience, renders more plausible the term *heroic* virtue, which is the sign of a holy life in the Christian tradition.

All Christians must be holy in the context of their vocations, the roles they play in society and Church. Of course, particular elements in the actual constitution of the holiness of each person will vary according to the particular conditions and circumstances, the situation, of that person. For this reason saints play an important role in the Church. They illustrate not only the gracious gifts of God. They also illustrate the myriad responses of persons to this grace in different times and places. What Christian holiness is revealed in the life of Jesus and his saints? They are the initiators and creative exemplars of precisely that holiness which is required by and proper to any given age. Explicitly canonized saints are but more eye-catching manifestations of the holiness that is possible and actual among many other people in the Church and the world whose "anonymous" holiness is celebrated on their own special feast day on November 1, All Saints. Living saints among the various members of the "simple" laity exert a powerful leadership within their particular contexts; for they effectively lead others to the experience of God's true goodness for human beings. God leads us to himself through and in them. The power of his grace within them enlightens our way to God. Their love of God enlightens our reading of the Sacred Scriptures, which cannot be properly appreciated apart from such love.

The tendency to identify Christian perfection with monasticism can be seen in the type of person chosen for canonization. From 1587, when the process of canonization was entrusted to the Congregation of Rites, until 1965, of the 238 persons canonized, only four could reasonably be considered to have lived a recognizably lay life. Of 1,171 persons beatified, a mere five were honored solely because of their lives as laity. Of 337 saints whose feasts were celebrated in the Tridentine Missal, 220 were either in orders or the monastic life or both. Of the remainder, many were known only by name, if they were historical figures at all, and very few lived a style of life recognizably similar to that of the vast majority of lay Christians. In the current Missal, commemorations are provided for 149 saints who lived after New Testament times. Of the 29 lay persons so commemorated, thirteen are early Roman martyrs, the details of whose lives are unknown, six of these being traditionally represented in iconography as consecrated virgins.

The martyrs and saints bear witness to the self-giving of Jesus that is operative in their lives. The Church believed that the martyrs had no need of purgation because by utterly giving themselves, they had attained the fullest potentialities of their existence, inasmuch as they utterly transcended selfness in fully accepting the Holy Spirit of Christ and his Father. The Church eventually recognized that there are ways of theocentric and Christocentric self-transcendence other than accepting physical death that may be to no less a degree the expression of the same love that is in Jesus and the triune communion. The contrast between the fulfillment attained by theocentric and Christocentric self-transcendence and the illusory fulfillments sought within the narrow limits of self-regarding concern is expressed in the question: ''What does a man gain by winning the whole world at the cost of his true self?'' (Mark 8:36).

Through participation with Christ and his body in the triune communion, we look beyond the limits of our own self, transience, and mortality for the master concern of our life; we transcend the superficiality of those ambitions on which human energies are wasted in the quest for an illusory security; we avoid the self-distortion that comes from making pleasure or self-aggrandizement the leading concern of our existence. The Father's love that motivated Christ's self-abandonment or self-giving is given to us in their Holy Spirit to liberate us *from* the obstacles that our endless forms of self-idolatry put in the way of any genuine love for God and all human persons. That love which is life eternal in the triune communion frees us *for* loving all others invincibly and irrevocably. The saints enjoy God's freedom for loving. They are not their own little gods, manipulating others for their own self-interest; rather they are epiphanies or glimpses of God's freedom in human life stories, the friends of God.

The measure of heroism and Christian living is very much the degree in which we can go beyond self-interest in seeking the true good of others. Paradoxically, in seeking a good that extends beyond one's self, family, community, and nation, one most enriches oneself and those who are close to one because all these lesser units live and have their being in the whole that is the world. In seeking the good of others, our own good is attained; a better world is a better world for everyone in it. The happiness and welfare of the individuals depend on that of their community, whether local, national, or global. The great biblical heroes were not detached and sublime members of an elite class; they came from, interacted with, and served the people; they were not men and women working out their private destiny as leaders apart and alone. Moses, David, Solomon, Peter and Paul, were all men struggling, erring, groping about in attempts to come to terms with their passions, their fears, their faith. Beyond their tenuous lives, and at the same time deep within them, was a caring presence—the only real hero, as it were—the God who was like a father with a child he deeply loves and to whom all those struggling humans were reaching out. The biblical heroes reflect a people's vision of the world; they tell us how people see the world and what they take to be the most important things in their lives. It is through our heroes that we tell one another who and what we truly are, whether in fact or in aspiration.

Heroes are something that we have willy-nilly, like sleep. We may sleep in a bed or in an armchair, but we must sleep somewhere. Heroes, too, we must have, consciously or unconsciously. Everyone has his or her heroes. The danger is that we may not have the

wisdom or intelligence or patience to select the right hero, the qualified leadership or ideal. There is always the danger of looking for
the person who offers simple and immediate answers to complex
questions. Throughout history, people have been susceptible to a
demagogue ready to lead them to some form of enslavement. We
do not understand complex issues and do not understand why it
is so hard for our leaders to solve them. Solve them they must. The
question is how to go about it. It is the question that challenges our
wisdom, intelligence, and moral sense in every age. The authentic
leader is our heroic response.

We cannot have human stories without heroes; therefore a narrative theology must be a theology of heroes too. It will ask questions about our vision of the ideal state of the world and of the ideal
conditions of life for ourselves—or in related terms, what role we
would like to play in the ideal scheme of things. Is the ideal positive end-state of existence something like an endless condition of
excitement, power, and applause, while the feared negative end-
state is something like one of routine and anonymity? Is the ideal
positive end-state a completely undisturbed life of stoic impassibil-
ity, in which life will not be agitated by anything as uncomfortable
as compassion or anger? Is the desired end-state one of omniscience
or omnipotence, of having everything perfectly under control and
in order and a corresponding intolerance of "messy" things, such
as feelings, friendship, anxiety? (Needs, defenses, and behavior are
pointers to the end-state desired.) Narrative theology will ask what
battles is a person fighting. What is the person in favor of? It is easy
to be general and negative; it is very hard to be concrete and positive. Some are led by bitterness and grudges all their lives. A strong
character or hero implies a person of strong desires. All motivation,
all action, represents some form of desire. One cannot learn without *wanting* to learn. What, therefore, does our hero want out of
life? What does the hero feel responsible for? What does the hero
do about it?

People can be happy only by doing *something*. What that something fulfills is needs or values; but people cannot just "be happy."
What do they desire and choose and commit themselves to? Our
heroes define themselves by their choices and attitudes and expec-

tations. A sense of identity in the original meaning of "identity" (sameness) means a constancy, stability, and therefore consistency in one's choices, attitudes, and expectations. If we say that we don't know who we are, we really seem to mean that we don't know what we want to do with our lives. The decisions, commitment, and expectations of our heroes express our own. In his *Spiritual Exercises,* St. Ignatius' meditation on the kingdom is an invitation to hero-worship, to make Jesus Christ our ultimate hope and aspiration.

In the Peanuts comic strip, Schroeder, with the bust of Beethoven on his piano, is a hero-worshiper. This brings out a difficulty in recognizing a hero. There must be the recognition of an objective scale of values, in this case those of music, and also the willingness to accept that somebody else is better at it than I am, therefore to be imitated. The same holds for the imitation of Christ in the king-dom meditation. One must also accept that, as with Schroeder and Beethoven, the worshiper will probably never be as good as the hero, so that the existence of the hero will always set limits to pride. So heroes are uncomfortable. Resentment, the worst deformation of feelings, is an idea as old as the story of Cain and Abel, the sibling rivals. The contemporary reluctance to accept heroes seems to be related both to rejection of objective scales of value, and also to unwillingness to admit that anybody can be better than I at anything. (Resentment attacks the value-quality that the superior person possesses, and the inferior not only lacks but feels unequal to acquiring. The attack amounts to a continuous belittling of the value in question, and it can extend to hatred and even violence against those who possess that value-quality).

Christian conversion, both as event and lifelong process, is a question of heroes. The Holy One of God, Christ, is the hero of the Christian community of faith. The saints are also venerated for their participation in the life of Christ. They, too, are heroes whose lives are true images of the true goodness of Christ. The life of Christ and his saints entails the enlargement of our horizon in both the event and lifelong process of our conversion. Their lives embodied and communicated their horizon or vision. We know a horizon only after living in it. So every conversion is like the vocation of Abraham, a call into the unknown. The new horizon is less unknown, and less terrifying, if we have seen somebody else living it and being happy doing so. That proves that the new horizon is truly "viable." Our lives are transformed by our heroes or saints within the body of Christ and the temple of the Spirit. If we cannot do what we cannot at least in some way imagine, Christ and his saints are the living images that enable our believing and hoping and loving within the concrete particularities of our life stories.

As the living image and sacred icon of God (Col 1:15-20; 2 Cor 3:12-18), Jesus Christ orients his community of faith to decision and action. Images, dominant stories, and ruling paradigms both issue in and in turn help to mould models for action. Jesus Christ as "image of the invisible God" cannot be separated from the body, the community, of which he is head. Christ and his community together are the image of God in whom the fullness of the triune God is revealed. Jesus Christ is a living, present, interpersonal reality whom we cannot accept apart from his Father and Spirit (in the triune communion), from his mother and brothers and sisters—his true "flesh and blood"—who hear the Word of God and live it, and from all persons within the universal human story of which he is (within the triune communion) the origin and ground and destiny. He is the integrating image of the integrating, covenant-creating, and covenant-sustaining covenant God of the triune communion. Jesus Christ and his community *together* form the image of the community of divine persons who are integrating what they are creating. The sacred icon of Jesus and his community reveals God the Creator and Integrator of the universe of human persons: "By this all will know that you are my disciples, if you have love for one another" (John 13:35). The reciprocal love within the community of which Christ is head images that of the Father and Son and Spirit. The reciprocal and integrating love of persons living in the Spirit of Jesus Christ and his Father is the sacrament of God for the integration of all human persons in friendship. The image of Christ and his friends is the sacrament enabling us to hear the God who calls us friends. Christ, the image of the befriending God, summons us to participate in his life of befriending others without exception. Our image of the Master defines our image of the disciple. The universally befriending and integrating Christ is effectively the Mas-

ter of those who go and do likewise (Luke 10:37). His Word is historically heard where it is lived, embodied, and imaged. His calling
us friends is experienced in our authentic friendships. Christ is the
icon of a love that manifests who God is and who we are called and
enabled to be.

Heroes (models, saints, leaders) bear a word of hope for others.
We may inquire what is that word of hope and what does it cost
them in terms of personal suffering. What heroes seem to have in
common is that all suffered and all managed to find some word of
hope for others, of which the individual was the bearer but not the
source, nor even particularly important in the context of history.

Heroes (models, saints, leaders) shape and educate our basic faith
and hope. All persons live by a basic faith and hope, a primal force
in human life, seeking form, shape, definition, structure. Persons
become the objects and shapers of our primal faith, the driving and
creative inner dynamism of our lives. They orient us toward decision and action. Christ is the shaper and educator of our basic faith
and hope and desire, declaring that he is our way, our truth, and
our life. As "image of the invisible God," Christ defines what we
believe to be the supreme good of all human desire and aspiration,
liberating us both from despair as regards the fulfillment of our
deepest desire and from the presumption of wishing to be the
guarantor of our own fulfillment. As the sacred icon of God, Christ
shapes our conviction about our own worth and well-being in the
present and in the future; he defines authentically theocentric human
life and fulfillment.

We must have some hero. The important question is, what kind?
And where does our hero lead us? Our primal faith can be mis-
placed. Our heroes can mislead and betray our primal faith and trust,
leading us to self-destruction. The ruin of individuals, societies, and
nations can be interpreted as a question of the wrong heroes,
models, and leaders. Christ warned his followers to beware of false
messiahs.

Although risk-taking is not in itself heroic, true heroism entails
a selfless act with a degree of risk. The only way to avoid all risk
is to curl up and die. The achievements of civilization derive from
individuals who have accepted almost incalculable risk. When a sys-

tem of values becomes so important that people are willing to live by it and die for it, heroic figures are born. Heroes are the concomitant of a system of value and thought that has been embraced by an aggregate of persons. The hero is the lived action aspect of the value system. Ideals and values that do not give rise to heroes have not been fully lived, concretized, and revealed.

The Virgilian hero of the *Aeneid* embodies another dimension of heroism: responsibility. An overwhelming sense of responsibility for family, friends, and country motivates such a hero. He is a man for others, responsible for them, conscientiously rendering duty and reverence to them, risking his own interests and life on their behalf in utter selflessness. Such responsibility for others is heroic love; in fact, there is no genuine love for others where there is no responsibility for them. In this context, the Church's insistence that Christians work for justice and peace is implicitly a call to Christian heroism for the realization of the divine purpose in our times; and this mission cannot be achieved without a keen sense of responsibility for other persons, societies, and nations, which demands that we sacrifice our own self-interests and nationalism. We will never convince anyone of the truth of the gospel if we rely upon conceptual clarity alone. That truth is communicated when embodied in the generally anonymous heroes and saints of the Christian community, who have willingly accepted a life of sacrifice in taking responsibility for others. Heroes and saints are capable of accepting the cost of commitment to others. The crucified and risen Christ is the sacred icon of divine and human commitment in covenant love.

Heroism involves particularity and accountability. The hero (model, saint, leader) is answerable for doing or failing to do what anyone who occupies his or her role owes to others, and this accountability terminates only with death. Moreover, this accountability is particular. It is to, for, and with specific individuals and groups and societies that the hero must do what he or she ought, and it is to these same that the hero is accountable. The hero does not aspire to universality even though in retrospect we may recognize universal worth in the hero's achievements. If Jesus is the Christian hero who saved the world, he did so by accepting his historical mission within the defined, limited world and culture of his native

Palestine, in obedience to his Father's will. Jesus was willingly and joyfully accountable to his Father for all that he said and did. He demanded that his followers be equally accountable to God for their lives with the same spirit of faith and trust. He called for the same total commitment or accountability to God that would inevitably entail our sharing his way of the cross: "If anyone wants to be a follower of mine, let him renounce himself and take up his cross daily and follow me" (Luke 9:23).

Heroes always have to do with the complexity of the concrete and the particular. They discover in the particular configuration of concrete circumstances that make up their lives what has to be done, and they do it. There is no antecedent blueprint in a book somewhere, simply to be copied or imitated. The simplicity of the hero is always an achievement; for the simplicity that really counts is that which is earned by mastering complexity. The hero does not retreat from the challenge of complexity to seek comfort in naive and sentimental fantasies of utopian simplicity. History is merciless toward those who flee complexity. History demands that complexity be contended with, and that simplicity be earned in it. The hero does not pretend that complexity is an illusion to be conquered by turning away from it. Will power alone does not simplify complexity. Freedom is more than doing what we please; it is the capacity for doing what is called for within the wearying and concrete complexity of adult life. That capacity entails love; for things must be loved first and improved afterwards. Love motivates the hero with the courage to confront complexity responsibly and hopefully.

The lives of our heros (models, saints, leaders) embody a story whose shape and form depends on what is counted as harm and danger and upon how success and failure, progress and decline, are understood and evaluated. To answer these questions will also explicitly and implicitly be to answer the question as to what we deem to be virtues and vices. Our heroes presuppose that we can win or lose, save ourselves, or go to moral destruction, that there is an order which requires from us the pursuit of certain ends and provides our judgments with the property of truth or falsity.

The fortitude of Christ, *the* Christian hero, is not divorced from the prudence that is able to recognize the elements of life as they really are and to translate this recognition into resolution and action.[2] It is not the recklessness of those unable to love anything or anyone; it is not the rashness of those who make a false evaluation of danger. It consists, rather, in Christ's steadfastness, in his total and invincible commitment to God in the service of others. The violence of his death, the savagery of his executioners, the darkness and the earthquake combined to form the apocalyptic moment when Christian faith recognized its Hero: "Meanwhile the centurion, together with the others guarding Jesus, had seen the earthquake and all that was taking place, and they were terrified and said, 'Truly this was the Son of God' " (Matt 27:54). Christian faith experiences its Hero as the light seen in the darkness that covers the earth; in fact, such faith is a way of seeing in the darkness of the human condition, for the Father has given us the Spirit of his Son (Gal 4:6) to confront it. The Christian community is united in the conviction that the Spirit of the Son's invincible love given to us will prevail over the powers of darkness and can achieve something of Christ's heroism in all of us.

CHAPTER TEN

The Church: Icon of the Trinity

The body of Christ is the icon of the triune God in John's account of Mary and John at the foot of the cross (19:25-30). The crucified Christ incorporates his mother and beloved disciple into his life by giving them his Spirit (19:30). The Father lives in Jesus (14:10). Jesus can give that life, the Holy Spirit of the Father (14:16, 26; 15:26), because he possesses it. As the Father loves the Son, the Son loves the disciples (15:9). The Holy Spirit, the life and love of the Father and Son, in the gift of the Father and Son to Mary and John, the beloved disciple, enabling them to fulfill the demand/call of the Father and Son to remain in their love (15:9, 12, 17). The Father loves them for loving his Son (16:27) because his Holy Spirit lives/loves in them. Through the gift of the Holy Spirit of the Father they are in communion with the Father in loving the Son. The Holy Spirit is equally the gift of the Son through whom they are in communion with the Son in loving the Father.

The farewell discourse at the Last Supper not only discloses the eternal life and love relationship of the Father and the Son but also the divine demand/call that we enter into that relationship. Jesus promises us that the Spirit of that eternal life and love will dwell with us forever (14:16-17, 25-26; 16:7-15), or, in still fuller words, the Trinity will draw us into its triune communion through the efficacy of his death and resurrection (14:23). From the moment when God pitched his tent in the camp of his people (1:14), to the great vision of the Apocalypse (21:1-4), John's Good News is that God dwells among us as the ultimate fulfillment of all human life. The triune community of divine love/life, we already know from 13:35, is manifest and communicated in the loving reciprocity of the disciples/ body of Christ. Our living in the Holy Spirit of the triune love/life fulfills the demand/call for reciprocity (15:17) that both the Father and Son enable us to fulfill through their self-communication in the gift of their Holy Spirit. The Father and Son come to us and dwell among us in their Holy Spirit, creating and sustaining the community or body of Christ as the icon of their triune life/love for the world.

In the scriptural iconography of the Gospel of John we "see" the triune God in the body of his crucified Son pouring out his life/love for all humankind. When the crucified Son bows his head and gives up his spirit (19:30) we "see" the Father and the Son (14:9) giving us their Holy Spirit, sharing the life/love of the triune communion with all humankind, enabling us to have in their eternal communion a relationship with one another that death itself cannot destroy. The eternal communion of the Father and Son is both seen and communicated in the crucified body of Christ that draws Mary and John together in the reciprocity of mother and son. The Father who eternally pours himself out in selfless, self-giving love is seen in the icon of the triune God, in the human self-giving love of his Son, pouring out their Holy Spirit to draw all humankind together within the loving reciprocity of the triune communion. The Son who eternally welcomes the selfless, self-giving love/life of his Father is seen in the icon of those who welcome that same love/life, the Holy Spirit of the triune communion recognized in the mutual love of the disciples (13:35). The Holy Spirit of the Father and Son is "seen" in the self-giving and welcoming love that forms the body of Christ, the icon of the triune communion.

Jesus Christ expresses and communicates the grace and demand, the gift and call, of the triune God for life within the triune communion. He is the icon of the God who both gives his love and calls for reciprocity in communion. If God is love, that love has its demands or commandments (e.g. 14:15, 21; 15:10, 12, 17). Jesus commands his disciples to love one another (15:17); he tells his mother to make John, the beloved disciple, her son; he tells his disciple to make Mary his mother. He enables them to meet the demands of God's love by giving them his life/love, the Holy Spirit of the Father and the Son. He calls them to the life that he enables them to live as the members of his body and the heirs of his Spirit.

As members of the body of Christ, Mary and John are central figures in John's scriptural iconography of the triune God. To see the Son commending his mother and beloved disciple to one another and giving up his spirit is to see the Father offering all humankind life in the triune communion through/in the body and Spirit of his Son. The Son's love for his heavenly Father and human mother integrates humankind within the life of the triune communion. The love that proceeds from the Father is the Son's love for both his Father and human mother/humankind.

When Jesus begins his mission at the wedding feast of Cana, he tells his mother to leave him alone because his hour has not come (2:4). When Jesus completes his mission on Calvary, his hour has come for the revelation of the deepest meaning of his relationship with his mother. When the cross manifests completely the Father's love for humankind, the ultimate meaning and fulfillment of Mary's maternity is revealed in the birth of the new family of God. Jesus shares with all humankind the life that he receives from his heavenly Father and human mother, making good his promise that when he was lifted up on the cross he would draw everyone to himself (12:32). The interpersonal life of Jesus Christ integrates humankind with the triune God in the triune communion. He communicates the life/love/Holy Spirit of the triune communion through and in his divine filial relationship with his Father and his human filial relationship with his mother. He is the integration of the triune God and humankind that he enables and demands. With filial love he welcomes the divine life of his Father and the human life of his mother, and he pours out that life for the ultimate fulfillment of all human life in the triune communion. Every beloved disciple is called to welcome that same life and share it with all others, just as Jesus welcomes and shares it. Our incorporation into the life of Christ gives us a direct share in his mission. Communion with God through Christ in the Holy Spirit makes us sharers in the life of each other, in the communion of the saints, a communion that transcends death itself.

John interprets the death of Jesus not only as the continuation of the life of Jesus (". . . having loved his own who were in the world, he loved them unto the end" (13:1), but also as its climax and culmination: "Greater love than this no man has, than that he lay down his life for his friends" (15:13). By interpreting the death of Jesus as the culmination of his life, John is saying that in his death Jesus was most alive, that Jesus was most alive in the giving of his life. The crucified Christ for John is an icon not of death, but of life even in death. John can assert this paradox of life and death from two perspectives. First, in giving his life, Jesus gave not this or that part of himself, but his whole self, his whole interpersonal life with his divine Father and human mother. There is nothing more that he could give. Laying down the fullness of his divine and human life in the triune communion for his friends is the greatest act of giving, the greatest act of divine and human love.

But it is also the greatest act of love from a second perspective. Jesus' act of giving is final and complete. It is a giving with no taking back. He gives the fullness of his interpersonal life in the triune communion in the most complete and final way. From both perspectives John can interpret the death of Jesus as the climax and culmination of his life, as the moment when he was most alive. Loving "unto the end" means not just to the final moment, but to the very limits of which love is capable. For John, then, Jesus was not passive in his dying, and his death was not just something inflicted on him. As seen by John, Jesus, in his death as an act of self-giving, reached that moment in his life when he was most active, most personal, most free. The death of Jesus was an act of living/loving, not an act of dying. It was an affirmation of life in the triune communion even in the face of death. This theme is at work in John's story of the Good Shepherd, who lays down his life for his sheep "that they may have life, and have it abundantly" (10:11). This is a clear allusion to and interpretation of the death of Jesus as the fullness of his self-giving for others.

The communion of the Christian community reveals and communicates the Holy Spirit of the self-giving Father and his self-giving Son integrating humankind within the triune communion of the triune God. Christ crucified is the icon of the loving outpouring of divine and human life in the reciprocity that constitutes such communion (koinōnia). He is the icon of the divine and human selflessness in communion with all divine and human others, willingly paying the price that such communion entails. There can be no communion (koinōnia) without selfless self-giving (kenōsis). Death itself cannot quench the invincible Spirit of love that is the eternal life of the Father and Son in the triune communion. That Spirit is always a gift, the triune God's self-gift and call to our real selves in the fullness of divine and human life with all others, enabling us to do and become what would otherwise be humanly impossible. Because God alone fully loves all others, good and evil, only the gift of his Spirit enables us to love all others with the love that no human evil or death itself can quench.

Our receiving the Holy Spirit of the triune God is not passive. The mother and faithful disciple stand by the crucified Christ, actively welcoming his love commandment and the gift of his enabling Spirit. We are never more fully alive and intensely active than when we love God with our whole heart and mind and soul and our neighbor as ourselves within the triune communion enabling such love. The Christian community, the body of Christ, is the living icon of the triune God when it stands faithfully by its crucified Lord, actively welcoming the gift of his Spirit in obedience to his call to the fullness of life in the triune communion. The gift of the Spirit enables the Christian community to follow its crucified and risen Lord's way of the cross, the way of selfless, self-giving love that culminates in the resurrection of the just for the fullness of life in the kingdom of the triune God. Our ongoing Christian conversion (metanoia) means our learning in the Spirit of Christ to become self-bestowing persons (kenōsis) serving others (diakonia) for the fullness of life in the triune communion (koinōnia).

Living Icons of Hope and Love

God speaks his word of hope and love in living icons, images or efficacious signs ("sacraments") that move our hearts and enlighten our minds. We cannot do what we cannot, at least in some way, imagine. We cannot believe, hope and love—our most significant "doing"—without enabling icons. We cannot perform the deeds of faith and hope and love without living icons or images that orient us to action. The eternal Word became flesh in the perfect image or icon of God that is Jesus Christ to transform all human hearts and minds, enabling us through the gift of his Spirit to love and hope in God above all and our neighbor as ourself. Jesus Christ and his body (Church) are the effectively transforming icon of God's creative and sustaining and predestining love for humankind, enabling our responding love and faith and hope. The Christian community affirms that it has seen or experienced the "glory" of God in his perfect image (icon), Jesus Christ; for "glory" is the impact of God's active presence transforming our lives. God's glory is manifest wherever his will is done or his love communicated, wherever we experience the transforming impact of his goodness.

The beauty of God's perfect image (icon) in Jesus Christ, according to the Greek Fathers, redeemed us by the impact of its powerfully transforming beauty, drawing us away from all moral and spiritual ugliness by attracting us to the Father. We are drawn to the fullness of life in God by the powerful attractiveness of living icons who concretely manifest his true goodness. The friends of God are the manifestations of his beauty, the glory or impact of God in human life stories. They are living icons in which God in love transcends even his transcendence through his real presence and activity in time and space; their true goodness, or "godliness," attracts us to God in faith and hope and love. We experience the goodness, trustworthiness, and credibility of God in and through the beauty of his living icons. We "know" God, in the biblical sense of personally experiencing his goodness, in our true love for one another; we know the Spirit of the Father and Son in such love, enabling us to affirm that God is love.

As living icons of hope and love, we share Jesus Christ's transforming and redemptive life; for images are orientations to decision and action. Our heroes, models, saints, and leaders are our images of what we should like to be. The images that we have of ourselves, others, and God shape our lives. It is important that these images be true, for they determine how we think and feel and act in our basic relationships with ourselves, others, and God. Living icons of hope and love are a word of hope and love for others who may

126 / SELF-GIVING AND SHARING

well envision themselves as little more than particles of dust lost in a meaningless void.

The crucified Christ is the Christian icon of hope and love, radically distinguishing Christianity from other religions with a unique way of thinking and feeling and acting with regard to ourselves, others, and God. Muslims, for example, cannot believe that God would ever allow a true prophet to be crucified. Because they accept Jesus as a true prophet, they believe that the crucifixion was a mere illusion. Their God does not allow such things. The cross is a scandal to all for whom it is blasphemous to affirm that God should become man, to experience human limitation, suffering, disgrace, and death itself; it is nonsense to the Greeks, whose Zeus is a detached spectator of human follies, a self-indulgent and fickle deity with no heart of compassion for humankind. The Greek icon of God in Zeus, understandably, has never won the hearts and minds of people to establish the basis for a world religion. The icon of God that is the crucified Christ continues to shape the lives of hundreds of millions, after two thousand years, with the conviction of God's boundless compassion for all humankind. The crucified Christ inspires hope and love despite our limitations, suffering, moral evils, and death itself. The crucified and risen Christ is the icon of God's unquenchable or undying love for everyone, shaping our conviction that God is eternal life and love, forever pouring out his life and love for us, investing his life in ours, and transforming us into living icons of his life and love. The sacred icon of the crucified is the matrix for our heartfelt conviction of our God-given goodness and dignity; for the Son of God is always giving his eternal life and love for us, transforming our image of ourselves, others, and God, enabling us to thank God both for being the God that he is and for the gift of every human life. We exist because God loves us; we continue to be because his love never ceases. (The song title "You're Nobody Till Somebody Loves You" rather captures this idea.) In the light of the sacred icon of the crucified Christ we see each person as a unique expression of God's thinking and loving. No one exists apart from that originating and sustaining and predestining divine thinking and loving, that divine knowledge and will. In the light of the crucified, we envision ourselves and all others as the continual recipients of God's all-embracing, integrating love, sharing the same origin and ground and destiny.

The Church employs its scriptural iconography for helping us to form a true image of God and ourselves and thereby to become living icons of hope and love. True love is always based on the truth about ourselves, others, and God. The Church cultivates such love through the use of its scriptural iconography as the basis for responding love to the One who has first shown love to us. Scriptures express the distinctive way that we have been loved by God in Christ and how we are empowered and required to love others in the same way. Scripture's witness to that love shapes the heart and schools the affections by presenting various images/icons for approaching God and a narrative that orders them into a pedagogical unity for learning to know God, in the biblical sense of doing his will or responding to his love. We are invited, for example, to address God as "Abba" (Luke 11:1-4) because the love of Jesus for God is the particular filial affection for the Father; this is the relationship into which he invites his followers when he lets them share his prayer. This scriptural iconography evokes a particular way of standing before God with Christ and others, a disposition of the heart and mind.

The Church's scriptural iconography serves as a matrix for the development of Christian life at every level: intrapersonal, interpersonal, social, national, and international. It is employed to foster prayerful contemplation and meditation, critical theological reflection, moral responsibility, and social commitment. The Church employs it to free us from false and distorted images of ourselves and God that orientate us to self-destructive behavior. Christ redeems our images. The Church as the body of Christ and temple of his Spirit transforms our lives by transforming our images through its scriptural iconography. Our prayerful reading and study of Scripture grounds our communion with Christ and his Body, orientating us to follow his way of total self-surrender to God in the service of others, transforming us into living icons of hope and love for all.

Conclusion

Jesus Christ is the living embodiment of the Good News, the sign of the kingdom, manifesting what human beings are like when they are under the rule of God. Similarly, his body the Church is the living embodiment of the Good News, the sign of the kingdom, God's new society manifesting, however imperfectly, what the human community is like when it comes under the rule of God. The Good News of God's purpose for all humankind is manifested and proclaimed in Jesus Christ and his body the Church where the Word of God becomes visible and the image of God becomes audible. God has manifested and proclaimed himself by sending his only Son: "No one has ever seen God, but God the only Son . . . has made him known" (John 1:18). So Jesus could say: "He who has seen me has seen the Father" (John 14:9); and Paul could add that Jesus is "the image of the invisible God" (Col 1:15). Similarly, the invisible God who made himself visible in Jesus Christ, continues to manifest himself in Christians when they love one another: "No one has ever seen God, but if we love each other, God lives in us and his love is made perfect in us" (1 John 4:12). To the extent that the body of Christ is transformed into a community of love grounded in truth, God visibly and audibly substantiates the credibility of his good news for all, opening the eyes of the blind and unstopping the ears of the deaf for the transformation of all humankind into a truthful and loving community.

CHAPTER ELEVEN

Communion in Beauty
and Beauty in Communion

Without the mature love that is capable of commitment there can
be no enduring friendship or community. The capacity to give oneself to others in friendship or in dedication is a mark of mature persons. A sort of inner solidity is necessary if a person is to have a
self to give others. Although immature persons may invest a great
deal of energy in trying to please others, their experience of true
and enduring friendship is rare if not nonexistent. They are superficial in their relationships. A superficial life causes frustration, and
compensating satisfactions may be sought in a number of directions:
in the search for power, in expensive tastes, in alcohol, or in ex-
ploratory sexual relationships. As Aristotle affirms, "no one would
choose a friendless existence on condition of having all other good
things in the world" (*Ethics,* book VIII, chapter 1). The incapacity
for friendship that seems to be common among those with serious
personality disorders could not be chosen by intelligently calculat-
ing selfishness. The pathological narcissists, who suffer from this
incapacity, do not really love themselves; under the mask of apparent self-love, there is a powerful if unconscious self-hatred. Revers-
ing both parts of the gospel imperative, such persons hate their
neighbor as themselves. The condition of the narcissist is notably
self-defeating even in the short run; it alienates others whose approval and affirmation is most intensely desired.

Insight into the narcissistic personality disorder implicitly contributes to our understanding of a mature and well-ordered love for oneself and others. The diagnostic criteria of this disorder, as reported in *Psychology Today*,[1] are: (a) grandiose sense of self-importance or uniqueness. The individual exaggerates achievements and talents, focusing on how special one's problems are; (b) preoccupation with fantasies of unlimited success, power, brilliance, beauty, or ideal love; (c) exhibitionistic: requires constant attention and admiration; (d) responds to criticism, indifference, or defeat with either cool indifference or with marked feelings of rage, inferiority, shame, or emptiness; (e) At least two of the following are characteristic of disturbances in interpersonal relationships: (1) lack of empathy: inability to recognize how others feel. (2) entitlement: expectation of special favors without assuming reciprocal responsibilities. (3) interpersonal exploitiveness: takes advantage of others to indulge one's own desires or for self-aggrandizement, with disregard for the personal integrity and rights of others. (4) Relationships characteristically vacillate between the extremes of over-idealization and devaluation.

Pathological narcissists, incapable of loving themselves, cannot give to their partners in a relationship; they are equally incapable of being satisfied with what they receive. On the assumption that human desire can be only partially fulfilled in this life, there always remains a residue of nonfulfillment, of difficulty, even of tragedy. In the face of this situation of partial fulfillment, the pathological narcissists focus their attention on the area of nonfulfillment in a state of constant resentment; and the most sure way to be unhappy is to make one's happiness dependent on the fulfillment of impossible conditions.[2]

Narcissism appears in the preoccupation with self and the decline of interest in public life and the common good; in the proliferation of therapies that declare we should be our own best friends, devote ourselves to self-actualization, and look out, above all, for "number one." It appears in the tendency of the young to eschew marriage and child-rearing in favor of remaining single, cohabitation, or living alone. In her essay, "The Meaning of Marriage," Jonda McFarlane affirmed that in the name of liberation and personal careers, too many young adults are living empty lives.[3] Feminism and the sexual revolution, McFarlane believes, confronted them with a freedom that they do not always know how to handle. Like many new Russian emigres, they often find it confusing and difficult suddenly to have control over their lives. When decisions concerning limits arise, they have no guidelines to help them. In some cases feminism, according to McFarlane, produced young women who— free to "have it all"—nearly killed themselves trying to do just that. Dramatically higher abortion rates and teenage pregnancy rates, as well as enormous increases in social diseases (and now Aids) resulted from the inability to set limits on sexual freedom. And now we have a generation so committed to success in the marketplace, or to "fun," that it puts off for years the commitment to marriage.

As a parent, McFarlane sees that so many of the young are not happier. What is often missing in their lives is a sense of values— and here parents must share the responsibility. Acquiescing in their demands for a less rule-oriented society, parents neglected to hand down the fundamental values they had learned in their time. Now the young have plenty of freedom but too little meaning in their lives. The basic tenet for finding meaning in life, according to McFarlane, is what it has been since civilization began: "Think of others." That means avoiding actions that could harm another. It means thinking of your work as something that makes a contribution to society, not just as a way to pay the bills. It means doing things that make other people's lives better.

Marriage both illustrates and reinforces the importance of thinking of others. For as long as there has been human society, men and women have recognized their need to mate: to establish a lifelong bond that provides the essence of the support that each human being needs as he or she struggles to face the challenges of life. Throughout history, it has been this union in which each partner is concerned with the good of the other that above all other forces has made it possible for men and women to experience their greatest joy. It is this built-in support system that enables them to be the best they can be. This sharing of life's best and worst times exponentially increases our ability to find meaning in life. Thinking back on our sorrows and joys, we realize that in both cases the first thing we do is reach out for the person we are closest to. Those who fear the commitment of marriage, who avoid the trouble and the responsibility in the name of more time, more money or more pleasure, cheat only themselves. Those who wait until they reach all their other goals before presenting themselves to a deserving mate often find their success empty. How much better, McFarlane concludes, to struggle *with* someone to reach a common goal, to be able to say, "We did it together," than to strive for one's own good.

Social critic Christopher Lasch describes the unloving pathological narcissists as chronically bored, restlessly in search of instantaneous intimacy, of emotional titillation without commitment.[4] They often complain of a sense of inner emptiness and suffer from hypochondria. Often facile at managing the impressions they give to others, they are ravenous for admiration but contemptuous of those they manipulate into providing it. Unappeasably hungry for emotional experiences with which to fill an inner void, they are tragically unable to enjoy life through identification with other people's achievement and happiness. Their devaluation of others, together with their lack of curiosity about them, impoverishes their personal life and reinforces their sense of emptiness. They depend on others for constant infusions of approval and admiration, living an almost parasitic existence. Their fear of emotional dependence and commitment, together with their manipulative, exploitative approach to others, makes their interpersonal life bland, superficial, and deeply unsatisfying. Their chronic uneasiness about themselves gives them a special affinity for therapy and therapeutic groups and movements. The shallowness of their emotional life, however, makes them resistant to successful analysis by preventing them from developing a close connection to the analyst. They tend to use intellect in the service of evasion rather than self-discovery; consequently, few psychiatrists take an optimistic view of the prospects for successful therapy. Pathological narcissists recoil from dependence on others, who are generally perceived as undependable and untrustworthy. The happiness of friendships based on the ability to maintain truthful communication eludes them. Although they may carry out their daily responsibilities and even achieve distinction, life often strikes them as not worth living. Pathological narcissists suffer from the incapacity to enjoy a genuinely interpersonal life based on a true love for others. Self-absorption frustrates their frantic search for fulfillment.

The inability to love is often masked by a veneer of friendliness or correctness characteristic of the passive-aggressive behavior pattern.[5] This pattern is marked by both passivity and aggressiveness. The aggressiveness may be expressed passively, for example, by obstructionism, pouting, procrastination, intentional inefficiency, or stubbornness. This behavior commonly reflects hostility that the individual feels he or she dare not express openly. Often such behavior is an expression of resentment for failing to find gratification in a relationship with an individual or institution upon which an individual is overdependent. Passive-aggressive persons are difficult to deal with because conflict never surfaces and they are unwilling to cooperate. They manage to maintain a rather serene picture of themselves as well-controlled, proper, nonviolent human beings. But they are not the peaceful or loving persons that they pretend to be. When they are confronted with the disruptive nature of their behavior, they do not easily give it up. Often they remain remote and inaccessible to healthy relationships. If any relationship begins to build, they quietly withdraw, leaving hurt behind.

A truly human existence is impossible without genuine personal relationships of reciprocal understanding and affection. The psychotic's world is an exclusively private world devoid of communion with others. It is the private hell of the deprived, demented, and diminished in flight from a world that they cannot control. The tendency to the ultimate inversion of self-worship becomes a source of inner conflict as external developments increasingly challenge a false self-image. In flight from the demands of truth for responsible decision and action, we secrete the life-lie, then live off the lie that we ourselves have secreted. Clinging to that lie is a fundamental option for self-deception and pretense. Withholding our true selves from others, we only frustrate our desire for their esteem and affection; for the true esteem and affection presuppose true knowledge.

If love means wishing the well-being of another, and if part of wishing that well-being is to behave responsibly toward another, then we must examine our behavior to ascertain whether it has unforeseen and unintended, possibly detrimental consequences for others we claim to love. Acting responsibly toward others is a prerequisite for showing love for them. There is a lack of love in the attitude that refuses to raise questions about one's own behavior.

Responsible parents teach their children to think of others. Unfortunately, many parents are not teaching "manners" to their children. Families have disintegrated in staggering numbers, and where there is still a mother and a father, both tend to be off at work, intentionally or unintentionally relegating the teaching of manners or thoughtful behavior to schools, day-care centers, baby-sitters or, as a final resort, the police. Living among strangers in neighborhoods that are not neighborhoods in the traditional sense, children are not inhibited or checked by the possible disapproval of their community.

Another reason for the decline in civility is that we now have three generations of people brought up on television shows on which most problems are solved by aggression and violence. Adding to this in the United States has been the general political climate, where the conciliatory tone of the Carter years was replaced by the tougher approach of the Reagan years.

Yet another factor is the change in the attitude of many women toward men and vice versa. The desirable American male role model of the seventies and early eighties was sensitive and vulnerable, a man who could shed tears and admit fears. Today's American women seem to be derisive of that model, preferring the tough guy—Rambo or Conan the Barbarian.

In sum, aggressive, assertive, even belligerent behavior is seen as strong in today's American marketplace of manners. Conciliatory, deferential, yielding behavior is seen as weak or contemptible. In a world where people do not have the thoughtfulness to say "you first," a world in which people are so frightened at the thought of being regarded as weak and uncompetitive that they do not have the courage to defer to others, civility wanes and the apes inherit the earth. The unceasing assaultive assertion of our rights in all those areas where generosity and gentleness used to prevail is a form of social decline rooted in egoistic disregard of others. As individuals not only develop but also suffer breakdowns, so too do societies.

Egoism is in conflict with the good of the entire social order. Up to a point, according to Bernard Lonergan, it can be countered by the law, the police, the judiciary, the prisons.[6] But there is a limit to the proportion of the population that can be kept in prison and, when egoism passes that limit, the agents of the law and ultimately the law itself have to become more tolerant and indulgent. So the good of the entire social order deteriorates. A civilization in decline, Lonergan affirms, digs its own grave with the relentless consistency of the absurdities that proceed from the inattention, oversight, unreasonableness, and irresponsibility of both individual egoists and group egoism.[7] If self-transcendence promotes progress, so the refusal of self-transcendence turns progress into cumulative decline. Consequently, Lonergan asserts that a religion which promotes self-transcendence to the point, not merely of justice, but of self-sacrificing love, will have a redemptive role in human society inasmuch as such love can undo the mischief of decline at both individual and social levels and restore the cumulative process of progress.[8]

Christianity is based on Christ's call to conversion (*metanoia*) from individual and social egoism to life in his Spirit of self-bestowal/investment (*kenōsis*) and service (*diakonia*) for the achievement of communion (*koinōnia*) with God and all others in the kingdom whose coming he proclaims (Mark 1:15). Learning to think of others, divine and human, is at the heart of Christ's program or mission for the transformation of humankind. The refusal to think of others, divine and human, is implicitly a rejection of the grace and demand of God in Christ for human fulfillment under the sovereignty of his love.

When we hear the Good News that God loves us and desires our love in return, we must have had some experience of true love and friendship in order to understand the Good News. We cannot have truly loved anyone, according to Aquinas (*De Veritate*, 22, 2 and 2m.), without in some sense having loved God; to have loved is the condition of coming to knowledge of God. Aquinas expresses in theoretical, metaphysical categories what John affirms about knowing God: "Everyone who loves has been begotten by God and knows God. One who does not love has known nothing of God, for God is love (1 John 4:7f.). That we can love only because we have first *been loved* is a psychological as well as a theological truth.

We are called not only to love God in others but to be also the media through whom God himself loves them. Christ's call to conversion implicitly demands that we accept his self-giving Spirit to become communicators of God's gift of love and friendship. His calling us "friends" (John 15:15) is God's grace and demand that we become friends. His "befriending" love enables ours, and it is operative in ours through the gift of his Spirit.

The befriending love of Christians is the "glory" or impact of God's transcendent love transforming humankind into the image of the self-giving Trinity. God's love transforms our memory of the past, our awareness of the present, and our anticipation of the future. It liberates us from forgetfulness of his past mercies, ignorance of his present mercies, and despair of his future mercies, transforming us into sacraments of his mercy for others. The success of Paul's and John's preaching about God's love is hard to imagine apart from the attractiveness of that love transfiguring their personalities.[9] The befriending God is known (in the biblical sense) in his befriending worshipers.[10] The God of compassion is known in his compassionate worshipers. God's love is not merely a loving attitude of God towards his people; rather, it is God himself, giving himself to his people.[11] The self-giving God is where he acts; in the self-giving of his true worshipers. The Giver is in his gifts; through them we have communion with the Giver himself (1 Cor 12:13).

True love, friendship, commitment, and community are related to beauty. Plato and the philosophies derived from him maintain that beauty is the quality that makes someone or something the object of possible love. St. Augustine affirms, "Only the beautiful is loved"; ". . . we cannot help loving what is beautiful."[12] If this is true, and if the old definition is also right: *pulchrum est quod visu placet*, to be beautiful means to be "pleasing to see"[13]—then there can be no true love without approving contemplation. In this respect, Mark's accounts of the baptism (1:11) and transfiguration (9:7) of Jesus, in which the voice from heaven affirms Jesus as the Beloved Son, imply that he is the Beautiful Son in whom the Father is pleased. Jesus is the Beauty of God incarnate whom the Father lovingly contemplates and approves. At the baptism the heavenly voice declares, "You are my beloved Son; my favor rests on you."

At the transfiguration a command is added, "This is my beloved Son; listen to him." The mission of the Beautiful Son, expressed in his call to conversion (Mark 1:15), is to make us pleasing to or beautiful in God's sight as partakers in his own pleasing beauty. God has "transfigured" our human nature in the person of his Beautiful Son, through and in whom we become his beautiful people. The self-giving love of the Beautiful Son has attracted, captivated, and transformed our minds and hearts, liberating us from the ugliness of egoism and pathological narcissism.[14] The beauty of the Beloved Son is the norm and measure of all true human beauty. In the Beautiful Son is the love of truth and the truth of goodness in which the Father is eternally pleased.

CHAPTER TWELVE

Finding Ourselves in
Communion with Christ[*]

When Jesus taught the crowds he used stories. This sometimes puzzled his disciples. Matthew tells us that they asked him why he used stories. Jesus used stories in his teaching not only to fulfill the Old Testament, as Matthew suggests, but even more basically because storytelling is the ordinary way in which we communicate with others. Imagine cracking up your car. Soon you will find yourself telling your story to your friends, your insurance agent, the mechanic, and sometimes the police and a lawyer. When applying for a job, you give your past employment history, the story of your working life. When you go for a medical checkup, they will look up your medical record, the story of your childhood illnesses and recoveries.

The storyteller is in the story. When we are telling a story, even a story about other people, we are also telling the story about ourselves. The stories we tell reveal how our lives affect others and how their lives affect us. When Jesus told stories, even stories about a woman baking bread or of a mustard seed that grew into a great tree, he was also revealing the story of his own life and the way his story relates to our story.

---

[*] This chapter has been coauthored with Thomas Cooper, with whom I coauthored *Tellers of the Word* (New York: Le Jacq, 1981).

The stories that attract us are the stories in which we see something of ourselves. Imagine a total stranger, perhaps someone you meet in a plane, who rambles endlessly about persons and events about which you have no knowledge or interest. That kind of storyteller is a bore. Imagine talking with someone you love. Everything—even the most trivial thing—is fascinating. What happens to her or him affects us; her or his story is part of our story.

Through Many Eyes

When we hear the story of Jesus, we hear the story of someone we love. What happened to him affects us. His story is part of our story; in fact, it is the heart of our story. Our stories make sense because of his story; his story discloses the meaning of our stories. Two friends were swapping stories about their childhood. One confessed that even from the start, Bible stories bored him; he saw no point in them. The other couldn't remember a time when these stories had not fascinated him. As he put it, "We must have been two very different children." Jesus himself tells us that no one can come to him unless the Father draws him. Our enjoyment of the Jesus story is itself a gift of the Spirit. Our attraction to the story is evidence of the Father's drawing power. When the catechist is telling the Jesus story, it is Jesus who is the storyteller.

Ordinarily, the first tellers of the Jesus story are our parents. God is disclosed, self-revealed through human storytellers. This self-revelation takes place both in the stories they tell about Jesus and in the stories their lives tell. There once was a theologian who invited some colleagues to contribute to a book he was planning. Each contributor was to single out the person or book that had most influenced his Christian formation. He expected his colleagues to write essays about Augustine, Aquinas, Ignatius Loyola, or some contemporary, like Rahner. One contributor surprised and disappointed him, for without hesitation, he singled out his mother. Her joyful and unquenchable faith, he affirmed, her hope and trust and love had been the basic and irreplaceable experience of the Good News about Jesus.

During the rite of baptism, the blessing of the parents expresses the prayerful hope that the parents will be "the first and best of teachers." Later, religion classes and, still later, courses in theology articulated and drew out the implications of a story that he had first heard in the stories told him by his mother. The story of her life was the story of someone who loved Jesus. The attractiveness of her life story was the means God used to draw him to the story of Jesus. An English bishop witnessed to the importance of such parental teaching when he spoke about the true meaning of baptismal priesthood, the priesthood that all believers share. Speaking to parents about their status as teachers, he remarked: "Compared to the priesthood that I share with you as a baptized Christian, my vocation to the episcopacy pales into insignificance."

For the inquirers, sponsors, catechists, and pastors are "the eyes" through which they are helped to see Jesus and "the mouths" through which Jesus' story is told. Each of these storytellers tells the story of Jesus in a unique way. Like the strands of a tapestry, each story complements the other stories so that together they make up one story, the universal story, which is at once the story of Jesus and the story of all humankind.

In telling the story of Jesus, human storytellers do not have total freedom. We must allow God, and not just ourselves, to shape the telling. There is a given content and meaning. We tell Jesus' story in our own words in such a way that it is the Word whom the Father will recognize as his own. Any telling of the gospel story, even though verbally correct, that fails to offer the hearer God's universal love distorts and renders it valueless. The Gospel story was created to elicit love. Like any created instrument, it can be misused or misconstrued.

The Value of the Story

Catechists should choose the right storytellers as models. In our search for models we should ask, "Is this person truly a friend of God?" In the biblical tradition, how seriously we take God's friendship is discerned by how seriously we take our neighbor's. If we cannot be friendly to the persons we can see, how can we be friends of the God we cannot see? The Christian community has recognized certain persons, the saints, as classic models for our storytelling. A second norm for discerning a friend of God is the presence of a willingness to suffer and to be inconvenienced in the telling of the Jesus story. We must be convinced of the worth of the Jesus story. Its worth does not depend on its hearers' applause. The storyteller must be prepared to suffer, as Jesus suffered, the incomprehension and hostility of those who have not welcomed the story as Good News.

When telling the story of Jesus we should not be surprised when others refuse to listen or reject what we say. In truth, if there is never any opposition to our telling of the Jesus story, it is wise to check to see whether we have watered it down. The Gospel story contains the kernel of answers to the questions that faith arouses. The catechist, at least in principle, already has some answers for which people are looking. The challenge for the catechist is to articulate the questions to which the Gospel is the answer: to help people make these questions their own. To parrot the commandments as a guide to living is useless unless we have asked the question "How should I live my life?" Likewise, a rote knowledge of the commandments of the Church will remain academic until we have asked the question "How should I live as a member of Christ's community, the Church?"

In a down-to-earth metaphor, Paul compares Christian development to the process of weaning. There is a kind of violence in forcing solid food into the mouth of an unweaned infant. Like newborn babes, we should feast upon the rich milk of Christ until we are strong enough for solid food. The catechetical role of the Church consists in presenting the inquirer with the whole Gospel of Christ in a digestible way so that the images of that story will enable one to understand the answer of Christ to the questions that a growing experience of Christian life will spontaneously suggest.

Catechists should not allow their understandable concern for preaching the Gospel effectively to cause them to become impatient with the apparent slowness of God to cooperate with our efforts. We should not look for instant results. The parable of the sower warns not to expect a hundredfold harvest from every seed; some will inevitably fall on rocky ground or among brambles. Paradoxically, we often reap what others have sown and do not live to see the harvest of our own planting. Even Jesus, the consummate teacher, died before seeing the fullness of the harvest. Questioning persons are not unwilling learners; rather, as Augustine reminds us, we would not be searching for God had we not already found God. Love seeks understanding. As we read in the Song of Solomon, Love asks all she meets where she can find her Lover. A loving heart is a questioning heart; an indifferent heart knows no such interest. When Matthew tells the story of Jesus' death, he punctuates his narrative with twenty questions. From the anointing of Bethany until the trial before Pilate, Matthew records for us both the questions of Jesus to his enemies and their questioning of him. Even the questions of Jesus' adversaries show that they are not indifferent and are, therefore, at least in touch with the love that could save them.

Throughout the Old Testament God challenges people with basic questions: "What have you been doing?" "Where are you going?" "Why have you abandoned me?" When Job complains about his sufferings, the divine Questioner does not offer explanations, but speaks out of a whirlwind: "I will question you" (Job 38:3). The climax of that book (38:41) shows God searching Job with a battery of questions about the power, the beauty, and the mystery of the created universe.

The Bible records commands, invitations, and warnings that God communicated to individuals and through them to the chosen people. But it also indicates that at times the Word of God took the form of a question. Isaiah, for example, recalls the questioning God that he experienced during his vision in the temple that brought his prophetic vision. He heard the Lord asking "Whom shall I send, and who will go for us?" (6:8).

In the New Testament the divine Questioner becomes flesh to dwell among us. In John the first words of Jesus form the question "What are you looking for?" (1:38). In Matthew the first words of Jesus occur when Satan tempts him to prove his divine sonship: "If you are the son of God, command these stones to become loaves of bread." Jesus counters the temptation by quoting Deuteronomy 8:3 about the deepest source of life: "Man shall not live by bread alone, but by every word that proceeds from the mouth of God" (Matt 4:3). In Luke's Gospel the first words of Jesus proclaim the

Good News: "The time is fulfilled, and the kingdom of God is at hand; repent, and believe in the gospel" (1:15). The God who says to Adam "Where are you?" (Gen 3:9) and to Job "I will question you" has come to us in human form to ask questions. In John's Gospel Jesus calls us into question before he presents his message. He wants us to examine what our hearts are set on, what we hope to discover and give ourselves to. We must ask ourselves what we are really looking for in life. John's Gospel invites us to ponder the questions of Jesus: from "Will you also go away?" (6:67) to "Do you know what I have done to you?" (13:12), from "Have I been with you so long, and yet you do not know me, Philip?" (14:9) to "Do you love me?" (21:15).

Celebrative Silence

One of the facts of life is that love thrives on conversation. When people can no longer speak to one another, it is a sign that love is dying, if not already dead. Prayer is the means by which we make our own the story of Jesus. In prayer we tell our story to Jesus, we narrate the events of our own lives, we tell him of our fears and hopes, and we listen to hear how the Jesus story resonates in our own lives. Prayer is the connecting act with Jesus as storyteller and storylistener; it is the interpersonal and mutual sharing of the life stories of two lovers.

The Second Vatican Council described the liturgy as the "summit towards which the activity of the Church is directed; at the same time it is the fountain from which all her power flows." The dramatic nature of liturgical celebration makes it a key element in the catechetical telling of the Jesus story. In the liturgy we bring to mind and make present the past and future moments of the universal story of Jesus: we proclaim his death until he comes.

The four Gospels record that Jesus punctuated his teaching and his telling of stories with periods of silence. These silences not only served to refresh Jesus and his disciples but also allowed time for the crowds to assimilate and make their own the teaching they had heard. These silences remind us that we always mean more than we can put into words. They put the words of Jesus into the context of the ultimate mystery. Prayerful withdrawal from the immediate concerns of daily life enables both the catechist and catechumens to be open to the mystery within and behind the story of Jesus and let it take possession of their minds and hearts.

A Holistic Approach

In *Tellers of the Word*, Father Tom Cooper and I attempted to write the first systematic and holistic theology of story. Drawing on a wide range of disciplines—psychology, history, biblical exegesis, and literary criticism—we found that the unifying notion of story and storytelling makes abstract concepts and terms come to life. We also became aware of the application of doctrine to human development. Discussing Christian living in our day, we tried to combine the insights of both the Christian and humanistic sources with a full and lively awareness of the former's revelation and tradition. After all, storytelling deals with the most basic drives and needs of human beings and it must be seen in relation to Christ and the Church. We felt that story would be a healthy antidote to a rigid conceptualism of moral categories that in the past seem to have reduced human values to a lifeless skeleton. Here we will briefly outline the practical implications of the book for catechesis in a catechumenate situation.

Before we can tell someone the story of Christ, that person must be prepared to hear it. When Jesus opened the ears and mouth of the deaf mute, he gave us a symbol of all Christian discipleship: the Christian catechist helps others to be open to hear God's Word and enables them to speak God's praise.

Tellers starts from the fact that people are a storytelling and storymaking lot. We are conscious of being persons because we are conscious of being the subjects of our stories. I know myself as the main actor in my life story. Like every story, my life has three dimensions—the past, the present, the future—and these are called to mind by my memory, my present awareness, and my anticipation of things to come. The story of every human life involves both a process (promise) and a term (fulfillment). We organize the way we tell the story of our life around the conclusion that we have chosen for our story.

If you imagine, for example, that the happy ending of your life would be one of married love, you will minister to those persons whom you care about and want to share such an ending. If you envision a life fulfilled by gospel ministry, you will entertain the possibilities of being ordained, taking vows, or living a life of service in the world of everyday affairs.

The art and skill with which we tell our stories express the artistry and skill with which we live our lives. Before we can make a story, we must be able to listen; we are storylisteners before we are storytellers. For example, the years preceding his public ministry, Jesus spent this reflective time listening to God before he publicly proclaimed his message. A human life is not exclusively a story of peak experiences. Patience recognizes the presence of God in ordinary and routine living.

Making the Story Happen

There is a craft to telling stories. Like any teacher or artist, storytellers use techniques and skills adapted for their purpose. The storytellers' art is measured by the ability to master complexity. The more they are able to unify within their stories, the greater their art as storytellers. The excellence of a human story is measured by the demands it makes of its authors. Storytellers are aware of the many varieties of authentic human experience. A good story is not just a story about oneself, but a mutual creation of the teller and the listeners. Both storytellers and listeners cooperate in making the story happen. Together they enter a world pieced together by creative imagination.

If storytellers and listeners are to create a story together, they need to speak the same language. At a deeper level, tellers and the audience must not only speak the same language but must also share a common language of images and symbols. When storytellers authentically articulate themselves as subjects of a human story (that is, as an authentic part of the universal story) they express the common subjectivity of men and women. Inasmuch as storylisteners make their own the story they hear, so do they enter a common world of meaning with tellers; together they create a world in which they can recognize themselves and ultimately come home to God.

As each story is a mutual creation of the teller and the listener, so every human life story is a mutual creation of the human teller and God. Every human story is coauthored by God and humankind. Inasmuch as God is the giver of all human life stories, they are manifestations and expressions of his love. They are to be judged and measured by the demands of his creative intention.

Of all the stories that God coauthors with humankind, the story in which God is known and revealed in the most normative way for Christian faith is the story of Jesus, the Word and Story of God become flesh. Every human life story will in some fashion reflect the presence of evil in the world and in human lives. The story of Jesus, the way in which he told his life story, redeems all human storytelling. The universal fact of sin results in the deliberate distortion of human life stories: we love to claim that we ourselves are the sole authors and centers of interest in our stories. We try to center the story about ourselves; that is, we take our story out of the context of the universal story of which God is the main author and listener. Because Jesus, a storyteller like ourselves in all things but sin, has centered his story within the true and ultimate context of the universal story—a story that embraces all human life stories and centers them on God. Because Jesus tells his story afresh in our stories, humankind's wounded capacity to tell and hear its story is redeemed and made whole.

In the Context of Redemptive Love

The way we envision God is always determined from the start by the way we love and treasure the things presented to us within the context of our life story. Furthermore, the way that Jesus Christ loved and treasured the things presented to him within the context of his life story reveals to Christian faith the meaning of authentic love and the true vision of God. The vision of the beloved sonship of God symbolized in the baptism of Jesus is further revealed as the foundation of the Christian story by Jesus' way of the cross. The story of Christ's life reveals the redemptive significance of suffering in every human life story. The way of the cross as disclosed in the story of Jesus reveals the nature of authentic suffering as a suffering out of love, because it reveals to Christian faith the extent to which the divine Storymaker is committed to the excellence of his universal story and his love for humankind.

This gift of God's love, a gift disclosed in the cross of Jesus and given through the sending forth of the Holy Spirit, grounds the story of Christian conversion. The four versions of the Gospel story given us by the evangelists serve the Church's catechetical purpose by functioning as four "manuals" toward Christian maturity. Mark prepares the catechumen for the sacramental celebration of the first moment of conversion in baptism. Matthew illuminates the way for the newly baptized to enter into fellowship. Luke, both in his Gospel and in Acts, helps the newly converted and communally strengthened Christian to enter into a life of missionary commitment. Finally, the story as told by John serves the more mature and contemplative Christian as a manual for discerning and attaining the full development of the Christian life as a life of sacramental worship and charity.

The Church employs these four stories as a means for communicating to new generations its foundational experience of the love of God in Christ Jesus and in his Spirit that has been given us. Basic to that experience of conversion is the feeling and the judgment that we are loved. The different ways of telling the story of Jesus correspond to the diverse ways in which God can tell us that we are loved. The central purpose of the Christian catechist in telling the story of Jesus throughout the catechumenate lies in cultivating this sense of being loved by other persons, both human and divine. This Christian conversion, the gift of God's love within our hearts, is worked out in a process of self-transcendence, in a lifetime's death in love and self-surrender to God and neighbor. The Gospel story evokes this Christian conversion both as an event and a process. The Christian storyteller, whether friend, sponsor, or catechist, is the means and instrument by which the Father draws persons to his Son and communicates to them the life-giving Spirit.

Jesus Christ is the sacrament who transforms human life stories. His life story is the outward and visible sign of the inward and invisible gift of God's love. The life story of the crucified-risen Jesus is the primordial sacrament of God's gift of his love, experienced by the Christian as underlying and informing all human life-stories.

The Gospel stories function as sacramental symbols evoked by the feeling for Christ of their writers and evoking the feeling of Christ of their readers or listeners. The resurrection of Jesus is the key to the Christian interpretation of the divine and human coauthorship of Jesus' story. It is a story that anchors and gives meaning to the story of the Church and the universal story of the world. Authentic storytelling creates a community of love and, consequently, understanding the Jesus story, the Good News, is conditioned by our participation in the living communities of Christian faith that tell the story. The tradition of the Church is the life story of Christians and to tell that life story is a central task of the catechist.

Jesus, the storyteller from Nazareth, by his life and death and resurrection, discloses God as Father, Son, and Holy Spirit. The blessed trinity and undivided unity of God, the community of divine persons that founds and is disclosed in all human community, must be at the center of all our storytelling. The Jesus story tells us that our own story finds its source, its direction, and its fulfillment in sharing the life of the Blessed Trinity.

What do we mean when we say "divine," "human," "love," "religious"? If we cannot indicate a single example of what we mean, we probably do not know what we are talking about. A new community—the Church—came into existence when the first persons pointed to Jesus and told his story to explain what they meant by "divine," "human," "love," "knowing God," "religious" and "just." They had heard the Question of God raised in Jesus, the Word of God; and because they had heard the Question within the depths of their being, they could recognize the Answer and proclaim it as the Good News that God is Love, the source and direction and destiny of all humankind.

CHAPTER THIRTEEN

Home, Homelessness, and Homecoming

Home, homelessness, and homecoming are elements of every biblical travel story, for each represents the spiritual quest for the origin and ground and destiny (= home) at the heart of every human life-story. Home is both a point of departure and arrival, the Alpha and the Omega, the basis for the dynamics of homecoming, of generation and regeneration, of birth and fulfillment. Homecoming is both a process, represented by the journey/travel metaphor in literature, and a term of arrival, rest, peace or Shalom. Home can indicate a way of being, when we say that we are "at home" with others. Home is primordially where father and mother are. Homecoming, in this context, means returning to our roots, origins, father and mother.

Adam and Eve were at home with God in paradise; however, their alienation from God rendered them homeless. Abraham leaves Ur, his original home, to find a new home. The Exodus of Moses starts from a place that is not an authentic home. Forty years of wandering and homelessness are sustained by the hope of a promised homeland. The Exile tells of a people driven from their true homeland and of their painful homelessness. The Exodus journey of liberation contrasts with the Exile journey into captivity, with the implication that home represents the utmost human freedom and that homelessness represents its loss. The return to Israel is seen as a new Exodus, the story of freedom regained.

The New Testament interprets the meaning of home, homelessness, and homecoming in terms of Jesus Christ. Luke's Gospel tells of the prodigal son's homelessness, alienation from his father, and joyful homecoming, with the implication that the fullness of human life is a question of being "at home" with our origin and ground and destiny in God (Luke 15:11-32). John's Gospel complements this notion with the affirmation that seeing Jesus is always seeing the Father (John 14:9). Jesus is always "at home" with his origin and ground and destiny in God; he is never alienated from the ultimate source and purpose of his life. Home is where the Father dwells and, as Jesus affirms, there is a place for everyone in his Father's house (John 14:1). His Father is everyone's true home or origin and ground and destiny. Because the Father makes his home in Jesus, Jesus affirms that all who love and obey him enjoy the freedom of being at home with the Father (John 8:31; 14:23). Communion with Jesus means being at home with our common origin and ground and destiny. Jesus is "the Way" home and "the Life" of home; for being with him is being with the Father (John 14:6f.), in touch with our real selves and at peace with a peace the world cannot give (John 14:27).

As we have noted, home is primordially where father and mother are. Just as all human generation entails a father and a mother, our spiritual regeneration in Jesus Christ entails not only our recognizing and welcoming our Father in him but also our mother. In John's Gospel we are not only told that seeing Jesus is seeing the Father, but also that the beloved disciple at the foot of the cross is enjoined by the imperative of the Crucified's divine and human love to recognize that "She (Mary) is your mother" (John 19:27). Our home and homecoming is implicitly a question of our communion with the divine and human authenticity of Jesus Christ, with his heavenly Father and human mother.

Just as Jesus Christ receives his life from his heavenly Father and his human mother, so too his body the Church is the family of God that is generated and sustained by the same life. The unique interpersonal reality that is Jesus Christ and his body the Church is the home of God and humankind, where the divine and the human are in perfect communion, love, peace, and reciprocity; it is the sacrament of homecoming, the self-gift and call of God for the fulfillment of all humankind.

The Father gives himself to humankind in his Son and their Spirit. Mary, in Luke's Gospel, receives that Spirit to become the mother of Jesus Christ; again, in Luke's Acts of the Apostles (1:14), Mary, in the company of the Twelve, receives at Pentecost the Spirit for the birth of the body of Christ, the Church. The divine Father gives himself to the human mother for the generation of Jesus Christ and his body the Church, the family of God. God's new creation, the generation of the family of God in Jesus Christ, is the work of the divine Father and human mother of Jesus Christ. The home that Jesus Christ is for God and humankind is a family, a communion that derives from the communion of the divine Father and the human mother of Jesus. As the son of both, he is "at home" with both. To see (love, know, obey) him is to see his Father and mother. He is that "home" where the Father dwells in humankind and humankind dwells in the Father. The Church is the body of Christ and the temple of his Spirit in which the Father dwells in a unique relationship with the mother of Christ; its life derives from both.

The self-giving Father and the self-giving mother of Jesus Christ are known in the self-giving of their Son that the family of God celebrates in its Eucharistic worship. Jesus gives his divine and human life in the Eucharist, the life he receives from his Father and mother, for the ultimate homecoming or integration of all divine and human life in the family (home) of God. The communion that Jesus is, is what he creates and sustains for all humankind. He communicates the communion (home) that he is in his body the Church and its sacrament, the Eucharist. The home of the divine and human that he is becomes the sacrament for universal homecoming in his body the Church and its sacraments.

Jesus Christ recalls the prophetic tradition of Israel that the Messiah would inaugurate eschatological happiness in universal homecoming (communion between God and humankind and among all humankind) through the formation of his banquet community (Isa 25:6-10; 55:1-3; 65:13-14). Even now the eschatological banquet community enjoys the home that the heavenly Father has prepared in Jesus for all who love him. Even now that community proclaims its home and celebrates its homecoming in its Eucharistic thanksgiving for Jesus Christ, who communicates the communion (home) of the divine and human that he is.

The integrating center of Jesus Christ's life of filial love for his Father and mother is that of the universal eschatological banquet community's eternal life and love even now proleptically celebrated in the Eucharist. The consummate integration and dynamic communion of divine and human life and love that is Jesus Christ unifies his body the Church even now in expectation of the fullness of divine and human life in the universal eschatological banquet community and grounds its conviction that we know God in what is authentically human and what is authentically human in God. The Father—the integrating center of Jesus Christ's life—integrates all humankind in and through him.

Biblical homecoming symbolism implies that human authenticity bespeaks a sound relationship with the true goodness of God, which is its ultimate measure. The truthfulness of authentic human lives evidences the truth of their vision of themselves, others, the world, and God. The beatitude of the pure of heart who see God is witnessed by the authenticity of their lives. The vision of the pure of heart who see God as he truly is, is born of God's gift of his love, which purifies the heart to see what it could not otherwise see and to become what it could not otherwise become. In his filial love for his Father and mother, Jesus enjoys and shares his vision of what is truly divine and truly human. He is the Pure of Heart in and through whom we see God and ourselves in communion, what we are and what we are called to be.

The Christian community recognizes, proclaims, and celebrates its divine and human origin and ground and destiny in its crucified and risen Lord's interpersonal life with his Father and all others. It recounts Jesus' affirmation that his life is poured out for the life of all humankind (Mark 14:24 = Matt 26:28) in the new covenant community, convinced that God is giving us his life in the flesh and blood relationships of his Son. The transcendent, invisible, and ineffable Father, through his Spirit given to Mary, has given us his perfect image or icon in Jesus Christ. Through his mother we see his Father. Through the flesh and blood of his mother, Jesus Christ is the human texture and icon of his Father. Similarly, through the Father we know the mother; for we cannot grasp the meaning of Jesus' interpersonal life unless the Father enables us (John 6:44).

Jesus' mother gives him his tradition, history, culture, no less than his flesh and blood. She heard the Word of God from Abraham, Isaac, Jacob, Joseph, David, Solomon, Isaiah, Jeremiah, Hosea, Joel, Amos, Ezekiel, and all her covenant brothers and sisters and kept it for Jesus. Jesus does not tell us about his heavenly Father apart from his mother's "flesh and blood"; in fact, he affirms that all who hear and live according to the grace and demand of God's word are his true flesh and blood, his family, deriving life from the same source (Matt 12:49).

Whatever Jesus Christ communicates of his Father is through his shared past and present and future with his true "flesh and blood." The Father speaks in the flesh and blood of his Son's intrapersonal, interpersonal, social, and historical life and body, the Church. He speaks in all that Jesus Christ is and that he derives from his mother. The divine speaks in the human. Jesus Christ hears his Father in his mother; he derives his life (divine and human) from both. Similarly, he hears the perfect harmony of his mother with his Father. To the extent that his body the Church shares that perfect harmony, we are enabled to verify the Word of God that "She is your mother" (John 19:27). The mother is seen in the human fidelity and commitment of Jesus Christ and his body to the Father. The perfect communion of the Father and mother in Jesus Christ's interpersonal life and body constitutes the home for the family of God and all human homecoming. Through the humanity of Jesus, through his body the Church, and his body and blood in the Eucharist, the mother together with the Father of Jesus is integral to the family of God.

Through the historical revelation of Jesus Christ, "the firstborn among many brothers and sisters" (Rom 8:29) of the family of God "every family in heaven and on earth receives its true name" (Eph 3:14). All the families of the earth are blessed (Acts 3:25) by the communion that his Father and mother have achieved in giving birth to his divine and human existence. Jesus Christ is the Good News of humankind at home with his heavenly Father and human mother. Through the communion that he is and communicates (home and homecoming, respectively), the divine and human are truly known and loved together in the family of God.

John's Gospel underscores the role of Jesus' mother in the family of God when he recounts that she is present right from the very beginning of his mission at the wedding at Cana (2:4) to the completion of his mission on Calvary, when the deepest meaning of her maternity is revealed in the birth of that family. Jesus shares his heavenly Father and human mother—the fullness of both his divine and human life—with all humankind, fulfilling his promise that when he is lifted up on the cross he will draw everyone to himself (John 12:32). Jesus gives his mother to his beloved disciple (and to all the family of God), who, most significantly, "took her to live in his home" (John 19:27). The fullness of the Son's divine and human love for his Father and mother is the life of the family that is his body and the temple of his Spirit, the home that the Father has prepared for all humankind's ultimate homecoming.

NOTES

CHAPTER TWO: THE LAST DAY AND THE LAST SUPPER

1. Mark's timetable reprinted from John Navone, *Gospel Love: A Narrative Theology* (Wilmington, Del.: Michael Glazier, 1984) 50–52.

2. Amos 5:18, 20; 8:9; Jer 15:9; Joel 2:2, 10, 16; 3:4; 4:15 and Zeph 1:15.

3. "Jesus gave a loud cry and breathed his last" (Mark 15:37) recalls Joel 4:16: "Yahweh roars from Sion."

4. The *Shema* is the Jewish confession of faith that Jesus, like every pious Jew, would have recited daily. It begins with the injunction to love God above all and obey his commandments. It consists of Deut 6:4-9; 11:13-21; Num 15:37-41.

CHAPTER THREE: CONVERSION FOR COMMUNION

1. The words "communion," "friendship," "fellowship," and *"koinōnia"* are used almost interchangeably throughout this article. For a bibliography on biblical *koinōnia*, see George Panikulam, *Koinōnia in the New Testament: A Dynamic Expression of Christian Life*, Analecta Biblica, 85 (Rome: Biblical Institute Press, 1979) 143–144.

2. Fraternal love constitutes a criterion of Christian fellowship in 1 John, where it is presented as a response to the love of God towards humankind manifested in the mission of the Son (1 John 4:9-10) and in making the believers the children of God (1 John 3:1). The presence of God is manifested in the love that the believers have for one another. See G. Panikulam, *Koinōnia in the New Testament*, 138.

3. To the extent that individuals, societies, and nations are their own "little gods," universal peace, love, and reconciliation are impossible; however, God has given us his Spirit to make these things possible. God alone actually loves and forgives all. Therefore, only by letting God be God in our lives can we actually love and forgive all. God's self-gift enables what is impossible without him.

4. Augustine affirms that we are restless until we rest in God. Jesus affirms in these parables that God is restless for our returning to him. If we do not possess our being independently of God at any moment, then the restlessness/longing that

we experience is that of our Origin-Ground-Destiny for us. Ours is the concomitant effect of the divine restlessness/longing. We experience at the depth of our being God's call for our return or the completion of his creation. Eternal suffering might be interpreted as the creature's experience of the Creator's unrequited love; for, as Aquinas and the Catholic tradition affirm, God's love for us is unfailing. Such suffering would be the experience of the unanswered call endlessly heard at the depths of our being. See "Home, Homelessness, and Homecoming," in J. Navone, *The Jesus Story: Our Life as Story in Christ* (Collegeville, Minn.: The Liturgical Press, 1979) 79–80.

5. See Robert Kress, *The Church: Communion, Sacrament, Communication* (New York/Mahwah, N.J.: Paulist Press, 1985). This excellent book underscores the importance of the Church as "God encountering the un-Godly." Kress affirms the triune God as the origin and pattern of the Church as communion (pp. 11–22).

6. See T. Barrosse, "The Relationship of Love to Faith in St. John," *Theological Studies* 15 (1957) 538–559.

7. See J. Navone, *Gospel Love* (Wilmington, Del.: Michael Glazier, 1984) 99–102.

8. Friendship, for Aquinas, is the aim of all human and divine law (*S.T. I-II.* q. 99, a.1, ad.2; *S.T. I-II*, q.99, a.2).

9. Every friendship between God and an individual is unique, because the love of God is received by unique individuals. Its expression is unique, because the active receptivity of the gift of God's love ever seeks expression among those who have received it. Although the receptivity and expression (= complacency and concern: cf. F. Crowe's three articles on these two dimensions of love, "Complacency and Concern," in *Theological Studies* 20, March, June, September, 1959) are the created effects of God's gift in us, they differ in that God works the first one alone, but the second along with us and in virtue of the first. We are his friends radically because all that Christ receives from his Father he shares with us (John 15:15); we are his friends authentically only if we respond to this communication of Love by faith and love, which means holding fast to his commandments (1 John 5:1–5). In that case, the eternal possession that God has of us is historically unfolded in a multiplicity of ways and persons.

The ground of this friendship is that "He has first loved us": being loved comes before loving, welcoming God's love for us is the source of any concern for his glory. This friendship must be lived out in the presence of the person to God, where the person is loved with an eternal love, where "those whom he has foreknown he has also predestined to become conformed to the image of his son" (Rom 8:29). The good news is that Christ summons us to respond to this predilection of eternal presence— our presence to God's eternal love and wisdom—from within our properly historical self. We never were and never are absent from God; however, God will ordinarily be present to many only intermittently, as a prevailing intention seeking varied and multiple expression, within the limits of the human consciousness' ability to sustain the presence of another. See David Burrell, "Indwelling: Presence and Dialogue," in *Theological Studies* 22 (March 1961) 16.

10. Paul Steidl-Meier, *Social Justice Ministry: Foundations and Concerns* (New York: Le Jacq, 1984) 299. Steidl-Meier treats of the unfolding of the interpersonal self in friendship (298–302) and of the unfolding of the social self in solidarity (302–305). Solidarity corresponds with Aristotle's notion of civic friendship. The unfolding of the intrapersonal self (297–298) is never privatized; even autonomous decision-making presupposes an interpersonal and social milieu. Individual development is not a pro-

ject of self-perfection. It is a gift and is based upon God's gifts and their inherent call to express ourselves in vocation, to be what God creates, calls and empowers us to be by identifying ourselves with God's will. The human personality develops genetically: as one continues to have new experiences, one will be unceasingly challenged to respond and to grow.

11. Fortitude is a dimension of the strong and enduring love of patience. The surrender of one's life for others is impossible without fortitude. We are more apt to honor the hero in the figure of the conqueror than in one who suffers. And since fortitude means precisely to endure "wounds" incurred on behalf of justice (from the loss of reputation or well-being to imprisonment or bodily harm), we are really looking, when we contemplate someone who has manifested fortitude, at the antithesis of the "conqueror." Such a person does not vanquish, but sacrifices. The ultimate test of the strong and enduring love manifested in patience and fortitude is martyrdom. Fortitude is the virtue of the seemingly vanquished, of the crucified Christ, *the* Christian hero. Accordingly, we are dealing with a falsehood in the prevailing notion of "hero," which distorts the essential qualities of fortitude. In the eyes of the ancients, the decisive criterion for fortitude consisted primarily in steadfast commitment and not in attacking. From the Christian standpoint, the steadfast love of the martyr has always been understood as a victory of invincible love and commitment.

12. J. Navone, *Communicating Christ* (Slough, U.K.: St. Paul Publications, 1976) 23. See Joseph Papin, ed., *The Eschaton: A Community of Love* (Villanova, Pa.: Villanova University Press, 1971).

13. The mystery of the Church is described in *Lumen Gentium* as a communion under three aspects. First, in the sense of biblical linguistic usage, it states that the eternal Father has created us according to his eternal decree and called us to participation in his divine life (*LG* 1). *Dei verbum* 1, 2 designates this participation as a personal community. *Ad gentes divinitus* 3 circumscribes the same matter of fact with *peace* and *communion*. *Gaudium et spes* 19 adds that in this *communion* with God the dignity of man and the truth of his being human consist in a special way. In the second place, *LG* 2 states that this communion, which is the goal of all salvation history, is realized historically in Jesus Christ in a unique way. He is the one mediator through whom God assumed human nature so that we might become participants in the divine nature; he is the epitome of all communion between God and man. Thirdly, what has happened in Christ once and for all is continued by the Holy Spirit (*LG* 48), who dwells in the Church and in the hearts of the faithful (*LG* 4); it is realized from within and propagated universally. The community with God realized by the Holy Spirit is the foundation of the community of the Church. It is the Spirit who unites the Church in community and ministry. Through the Spirit the Church is a communion with God, as are the members of the Church among one another. It is ultimately, as the Second Vatican Council said after the martyr-bishop Cyprian (see *De oratione dominica* 23: *PL* 4:553), participation in the Trinitarian communion itself. The Church is not only the image or sign of the Trinitarian communion but also its re-presentation.

14. Irenaeus of Lyons allegorically calls the Son and the Holy Spirit the "hands of God" (*Adversus Haereses* 5, 1, 3; 5, 5, 1; 5, 28, 1). Irenaeus believes that the Father is always at work in human history, shaping humankind into the image of the triune communion of the three divine Persons, because the words "Let us make hu-

mankind after our image and likeness" are addressed by the Father to the Son and the Holy Spirit. The Father creates, embraces, and draws all humankind to himself through his Son and Spirit. He draws all humankind with his two "hands" into the triune communion.

CHAPTER FIVE: THE GRAVES OF CRAVING AND THE EMPTY TOMB

1. I am indebted to Joseph Wimmer for calling to my attention the relationship, especially with regard to the Graves of Craving, in his doctoral dissertation, "The Meaning and Motivation of Fasting According to the Synoptic Gospels," (Rome: Gregorian University, 1979) 62–71, *passim*.

2. Walter M. Abbott, ed. *"Gaudium et Spes,"* n. 10, in *The Documents of Vatican II* (New York: Geoffrey Chapman & American Press, 1966), tenth printing, 207.

3. *Ibid.*, p. 215.

4. *Ibid.*

5. Otto Baab, *The Theology of the Old Testament* (New York: Abingdon-Cokesburg, 1949) 105, 110.

6. Richard Sennett, "Destructive Gemeinschaft," in *Partisan Review* (1976) 53.

7. Alekandr I. Solzhenitsyn, *The Gulag Archipelago*, III-IV (New York: Harper & Row, 1975) 615–16.

8. John Henry Newman, *A Grammar of Assent* (New York: Doubleday, 1958) 101.

9. Bernard Lonergan, *Method in Theology* (London: Darton, Longman & Todd, 1971) 116.

CHAPTER SIX: THE PERILOUS PROJECT OF COMMUNION

1. Benedict M. Ashley, O.P. explains in terms of natural law how Christ illuminates our historical experience, in "Scriptural Grounds for Concrete Moral Norms," *The Thomist* 52/1, (January 1988) 16: Moreover, since the natural law is known through human experience, and since the Jewish-Christian experience culminating in the encounter with Jesus Christ is the historically unique, integral, and ultimate self-revelation of God, the insight that this experience has given into what it is to be truly human surely must also be uniquely complete. The natural law is based on an understanding of human nature, but in a world of sin human nature is nowhere perfectly exemplified except in Jesus and his holy mother.

CHAPTER EIGHT: QUESTIONS FOR COMMUNION

1. Bernard Lonergan, *Method in Theology* (London: Darton, Longman & Todd, 1971) 103.

2. *Ibid.*, 105.

3. Frederick E. Crowe, "Neither Jew nor Greek, But One Human Nature and Operation in All," in *Philippine Studies* 13 (1965), 561–66. In this section, Crowe treats of biblical interest in questions. Crowe comments that questions may be introduced by the same interrogative and show the same grammatical form; but it is the *intention* of the questioner that determines the type of question: does he intend to put

an objection as one contradicting, as one concerned with the truth? Or does he intend to ask for explanation as one puzzled and desiring understanding. Crowe assigns Mary's question in Luke 1:34 to the latter type, the Lord's in Matthew 22:45 to the former, but this is for him a matter of exegesis to decide. Generally, he believes that questions put in sarcasm (John 1:46) or hostility (John 6:42, 52) intend to contradict and regard the level of truth, whereas a more neutral attitude such as that shown by the Jerusalem delegation to the Baptist (John 1:25) could pertain to either level. In fact, Crowe believes that the average person freely mingles both levels in confusion, and there is no reason for insisting that a given question must be a pure case of one or the other type (p. 564).

4. The life the risen Lord enjoys is the life his disciples are learning to enjoy in giving their lives for others. Whatever hope we bear for others will cost us something in terms of personal sacrifice. The suffering of dying with Christ is all of a piece with the joy of rising with him in that love which fulfills the Great Commandment. The mystery of the cross raises the question: Am I no more than a thirty/forty/fifty/sixty/seventy year old fetus? Have I ever cared for or inconvenienced myself for anyone? Or have I been so obsessed with a fetal need for security that I have never experienced the freedom of living or caring for others? That we are called to a fullness of life beyond the "fetal state" is at the heart of the Good News. (See J. Navone, "Hearing God's Word and Questions," in *Religious Life Review* 27/132 [May/June 1988] 144).

5. See Peter Drilling, "*Mysterium Tremendum*," *Method* 5/2 (October 1987) 58–72.

CHAPTER NINE: MODELS FOR COMMUNION

1. W. K. Kirkpatrick, *Psychological Seduction* (Nashville/Camden/New York: Thomas Nelson Publishers, 1983) 107, 119.

2. Josef Pieper, *Problems of Modern Faith* (Chicago: Franciscan Herald Press, 1985) 194.

CHAPTER TEN. THE CHURCH: ICON OF THE TRINITY

Peter Viereck, in his *Metapolitics: The Roots of the Nazi Mind* (New York: Capricorn Books, 1941), implicitly helps us to appreciate the distorted images and evil condition from which Christ redeems us. Spengler, Nietzsche, and Wagner contributed an image of the human person as a beast of prey for the formation of the Nazi mind.

. For Spengler the great beasts of prey were noble creatures of the most perfect type and without the "lies" of human morality due to "weakness"; whereas believers in social ethics were merely beasts of prey with their teeth pulled out. Nietzsche affirmed that Christianity aimed at mastering beasts of prey; its *modus vivendi* was to make them ill—to make feeble was the Christian recipe for taming or civilizing. Wagner believed that our clergy-ridden civilization reduced the health-exuding warriors of the north into weak-nerved cripples.

Nazi propagandist Alfred Rosenberg reinterpreted Christ as one of a long line of Aryan heroes ranging from Wotan and Siegfried to Wagner and Hitler. The Nazi state was believed to image and embody the totality of God; hence, Pastor Leffler asked people to choose between Israel and God as to which is the "chosen people" to embody the "God of History." Hans Kerrl, Minister for Church Affairs, affirmed in 1937 that a new authority had arisen as to what Christ and Christianity were really all about: Adolph Hitler, the true Holy Spirit. Fichte, a century before the rise of Hitler, had affirmed that the German mind was the self-consciousness of God. If our image of God determines the persons we become, our image of ourselves reflects what we believe to be the truth about God.

The Nazis' idealized image of the divine and human as predator defined them, implicitly corroborating the teaching of the prophets that the worshiper is assimilated to that which he or she worships: "Vanity they pursued, vanity they became" (Jeremiah 2:5).

CHAPTER ELEVEN: COMMUNION IN BEAUTY AND BEAUTY IN COMMUNION

1. Otto Kernberg, interviewed by Linda Wolfe. "Why Some People Can't Love," *Psychology Today* (June 1978) 58–59.

2. Bartholomew Kiely, S.J., *Psychology and Moral Theology* (Rome: Gregorian University Press, 1980) 228.

3. Jonda McFarlane, "The Meaning of Marriage," *Newsweek* (August 17, 1987) 8.

4. Christopher Lasch, *The Culture of Narcissism* (London: Abacus, 1980) 36–41.

5. Richard Dean Parsons and Robert J. Wicks, ed., *Passive-Aggressiveness* (New York: Brunner/Mazel, 1983) 6, 216.

6. Bernard Lonergan, *Method in Theology* (London: Darton, Longman & Todd, 1971) 54.

7. *Ibid.*, p. 55.

8. *Ibid.*

9. Thomas Cooper, *Cherubino's Quest: The Reasons of the Heart and Their Relationship to Mind in the Metanoic Theology of Bernard Lonergan*, unpublished doctoral dissertation successfully defended for the degree of philosophy, University of Lancaster, 1984, p. 285. This is a supremely good critical study of how divine love transforms human life at every level.

10. See James V. Schall, "The Totality of Society: From Justice to Friendship," in *The Thomist* 20/1 (January 1957), pp. 1–26. Aquinas conceives of charity as nothing more than friendship with God (*Summa Theol. I–II*, q. 99, a.1, ad 2; *II–II*, q̇. 23, a.1; and *III Sent.*, d. 27, q.2, a.1). Aristotle believes that even though friendship takes time and requires communication, we can approach every one of our fellow citizens as though he or she were a friend, as having the potential of being a close friend (*Nichomachean Ethics*, 1155a). Friendship is thus constitutive of a moral community that is indispensable to the formation of virtue and character. Communion and hospitality mark an authentic community of friends. Hospitality guarantees that communion does not become self-enclosed in tribalism, narcissism, and self-idolatry.

11. Peter Carnley, *The Structure of Resurrection Belief* (Oxford: Clarendon Press, 1987) 337.

12. *Confessions*, 4, 13; *On Music* 6, 13.

13. The German word *schön* (beautiful) is linked with *schauen* (to see); its literal meaning is "worth seeing."

14. The "ugliness" from which the beauty of Christ withdraws us is implied in St. Paul's "vice-lists" in Rom 1:29-31; 13:13; 1 Cor 5:10-11; 6:9-10; 2 Cor 12:20-21; Gal 5:19-21; and Col 3:5, 8. An alphabetical list of the vices assuring egocentric isolation dehumanization is presented by Jerome Murphy-O'Connor, O.P., in *Becoming Human Together: The Pastoral Anthropology of St. Paul* (Wilmington, Del.: Michael Glazier, 1982) 133-4: anger, arrogance, blasphemy, carousing, conceit, contention, contriver of evil, covetousness, deceit, disobedience, dissension, drunkenness, faithlessness, foolishness, hating, haughtiness, homosexuality, idolatry, immorality, jealousy, licentiousness, malignity, murder, obscene speech, pederasty, villification, sectarianism, selfish ambition, senselessness, sexual passion, slander, sorcery, stealing, swindling, tale-bearing, unlovingness, unmercifulness, unruliness, viciousness, wickedness. All these vices make genuine community and friendship impossible; they are ways people seal themselves off from one another and God for a "dog-eat-dog" condition that is genuinely "infernal." Joy and love go together naturally; so, also, misery and unlove. As misery loves company, so misery can be the root of a desperate search for pleasure. But the pleasure of the senses cannot be a substitute for joy.

SELECT BIBLIOGRAPHY FOR CHAPTER FOUR

Robert Kress. *The Church: Communion, Sacrament, Communication* (New York/Mahwah, N.J.: Paulist Press, 1985).
Bernard Lonergan. *Method in Theology* (London: Darton, Longman & Todd, 1972).
Jerome Murphy-O'Connor, O.P. *Becoming Human Together: The Pastoral Anthropology of St. Paul* (Wilmington, Del.: Michael Glazier, 1982).
John Navone and Thomas Cooper. *Tellers of the Word* (formerly Le Jacq, now published [1981] by Jesuit Educational Center for Human Development, 42 Kirkland Street, Cambridge, Mass., 02138.
John Navone. *Gospel Love* (Wilmington, Del.: Michael Glazier, 1984).
Jerome H. Neyrey, S.J. *Christ is Community: Christologies of the New Testament* (Wilmington, Del.: Michael Glazier, 1985).
James V. Schall, S.J. "The Totality of Society: From Justice to Friendship," *The Thomist* 21/1 (January 1957) 1-26.

DATE DUE